HELL'S HALF ACRE

Acknowledgements

Thanks to Parks Canada for its assistance with funding to help edit this manuscript. Thanks also to the Turner Valley Oilfield Society, the Glenbow Archives, and the people of the Turner Valley oilfield communities for their contributions to the Turner Valley Oral History Project.

This book is dedicated to the men, women, and children who lived near Hell's Half Acre.

HELL'S HALF ACRE

Early Days in the Great Alberta Oil Patch

David A. Finch

Heritage
House

Library and Archives Canada Cataloguing in Publication
Finch, David, 1956-
Hell's half acre : early days in the Great Alberta Oil Patch / David A. Finch.
ISBN 1-894384-82-2
1. Turner Valley (Alta.)--History. 2. Turner Valley (Alta.)--Biography. 3. Oil fields--Alberta--Turner Valley--History. 4. Oil industry workers--Alberta--Turner Valley--Biography. I. Title.
HD9574.C23A54 2005   338.2'7282'0971234
C2005-901003-7

Heritage House acknowledges the financial support for our publishing program from the Government of Canada through the Book Publishing Industry Development Program (BPIDP), Canada Council for the Arts, and the British Columbia Arts Council

Heritage House Publishing Company Ltd.
#108-17665-66A Avenue
Surrey, BC   Canada
V3S 2A7
greatbooks@heritagehouse.ca
www.heritagehouse.ca

This book has been produced on 100% recycled paper, processed chlorine free and printed with vegetable-based inks.

Printed in Canada

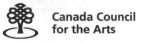

Contents

Introduction

The Story of Oil

"Thank you so very much for coming and talking to me," said old Alex Hartell after I interviewed him on his ranch in southwestern Alberta. "I've been waiting a long time to tell somebody my story." He died a few weeks later of old age.

Once upon a time people kept diaries, letters, and memoirs of their lives, but that time has passed. For most people, the events of their lives are mundane, even boring. But as they age and gain perspective on life, they sometimes realize that their stories have value.

It was this treasure-trove of experience, wisdom, and anecdote that I set out to collect many years ago. I first examined the social history of the western Canadian petroleum industry as part of the research for a thesis at the University of Calgary in the early 1980s. A research project for the Turner Valley Oilfield Society a decade later provided an opportunity to sit down with dozens of oldtimers, from every walk of life, and listen as they told stories of their lives in western Canada's first economically successful oilfield.

For more than two decades the stories of these people have fascinated me. Photographs added more detail, as did newspaper accounts. Articles and books have added to the storehouse of information as have other media including radio and television programs, even plays.

Hell's Half Acre takes you back to the original stories, to the kitchen tables and living rooms where these unsung pioneers of the oil industry told their stories. They are not the heroes of capitalism, but its pawns. This is the story of the working class.

Hell's Half Acre is a real place, in a coulee just outside the town of Turner Valley. For two decades companies piped excess natural gas to the lip of this gorge and burned it—in order to produce valuable gasoline they had to also produce the natural gas for which there were limited markets.

To this day the scars of the inferno that was Hell's Half Acre remain in that coulee. The ground is still scorched. In places it looks like porcelain, it was baked so thoroughly. That flare, and thousands of others like it, turned night into day for many years so when it came time to publish the local history for Alberta's 75th Anniversary, the committee called the book "In the Light of the Flares."

Gas burning at Hell's Half Acre, Turner Valley. (Glenbow Archives, NA-1716-5)

Chapter 1

Canada's First Gusher – 1914

Bobby Brown sat on his porch in a small mountain town east of Los Angeles in 1992 and told the story of his adventures in Canada. Born in Geneva, Indiana, on May 22, 1910, Bobby came to Alberta in 1912 with his family. His father, Joseph and his brother Robert E. Lee Brown, were "top oil drillers of Indiana."

"I was still in short pants the day the oil boom came to Sheep Creek, but 78 years later I remember it as if it was yesterday. From the little shack I watched the men drilling. Day and night, the bit at the end of a long steel cable pounded into the hole. Then one day the yard between the shack and the rig was full of cars. I remember the reflection of my face in the shiny hubcaps. Spokes in the tires looked like fingers holding the wheels onto the cars. Big fenders, running boards and round headlights all caught my attention. I was pleased. All these people had come to visit my house. But why?"

"We all loved Canada—my brother, Charley, and sister, Josephine. We'd come North with our mother, Mary, and father, Joseph H. Brown Jr., and uncle Bob Brown. After Calgary oilman Archie Dingman called Geneva, Indiana looking for drillers, things happened quickly and we were on a train headed north. At Toronto's Union Station we boarded the Canadian Pacific Railway's transcontinental passenger train. Hour after hour Canada rolled by, day after day of rocks and trees and water. Finally, we saw the prairies. We explored Winnipeg for a few hours, bought food, saw the sights. Then, with the steam engines belching smoke and sparks, the train raced towards the mountains."

"The Rockies came into view the next day, jagged, snow covered, a backbone against the horizon. But we got off the train in Calgary. The sandstone station looked impressive. Black porters unloaded our baggage. There to meet us, smiling from ear to ear, was Archie Dingman. He loaded us into his truck and off we went. At McLeod Trail we turned south, bouncing over the CPR tracks, up over Cemetery Hill and into the countryside. A few hours later we arrived in Okotoks, dusty from the gravel road. Then it was cross-country, following old wagon trails 18 miles to Black Diamond. Then we forded Sheep Creek and followed the valley west for two more miles into the setting sun. It was almost dark when we arrived at our new home. Finally, Archie drove us across the floodplain and stopped his truck by a shack, little more than a lean-to. Our family tumbled out and began life in western Canada's first oilfield. Two years later we moved on, following the oil booms."

"Canada was just one long adventure for my family. My older brother Charley quickly set up a trapline and hunted coyotes, ptarmigan and prairie chickens with a .22 calibre single-shot rifle. My sister and I stayed closer to home, helping Mom with chores around the house. I loved the cowboys the best, especially Davey Blacklock. He was my hero and he let me dress up in his sheepskin chaps when he visited. With no schools, neighbours, radio or electricity, we kids made our own fun. Local First Nations people, the Stoneys, visited often and we stared at the shy Native kids. There was also a puppy. Lots of families have pets and some of them even get in trouble. Our puppy developed a taste for chicken, but not for the leftover morsels from the supper table. When hungry, he took whole chickens, live. And why not? He was a coyote pup after all. So he ended up in a

Dingman #1 and 2 wells, circa 1916. (Glenbow Archives, NA-246-1)

box one day, skinned out, tanned and made into a stole for
Auntie Nora back in Indiana."

While the kids had fun, the men were hard at work. Drilling
for oil is tricky business, but the Browns were some of the best.
Joe Brown Sr., helped drill the discovery well in Titusville,
Pennsylvania, in 1859. That gusher made history and started
the United States on its way to become the biggest oil-consum-
ing country in the world. Men like the Browns quickly trained
younger men to build massive wooden rigs and operate the heavy
steam-powered machinery that punched holes deep into the
earth. The early drilling rigs were simple: they lifted heavy drill
bits and dropped them at the end of long manila ropes or steel
cables, bashing their way through clay, rock, water, and soil. Two
or three men ran the steam-powered rig in 12-hour shifts, around
the clock, until they found oil or ran out of money.

Compared to the American oilfields, the Alberta oilpatch
seemed a primitive place to the Browns. Mary immediately trans-
formed the crude two-room shack into a home for her family.
The children slept in folding cots in the main room. She cooked
for her husband, brother-in-law, and three growing children.
She also cooked for the construction crew until the oil company
hired a Chinese cook. Food came from Okotoks on the company
supply wagon. The Browns sometimes picked up a few things at
Blakeman's Store in nearby Black Diamond. By the time drillers
found oil in 1914, the village had telephones, stores, a blacksmith and a butcher, hotels and restaurants. Food spoiled quickly
without refrigeration at the wellsite in the summer, so men built
a cold box by the creek. Although the oil company furnished
meat, there was no local meat market to supply beef for Mary's
kitchen table. Members of a meat co-operative slaughtered an an-

imal every week and shared the animal. None of the meat spoiled and everyone had fresh beef.

Stoney Natives often passed through the area and they sometimes took parts of the animals the whites didn't use. Mary Brown quickly made friends with the Stonies. She provided them with food in exchange for rose petals and wolf willow beads. After boiling the rose petals into a mush, she rolled them into balls and let them dry. A hot needle or hat pin burned a hole through them so she could string them on a stiff cord with the wolf willow beads—a simple but beautiful necklace. More than 70 years later Bobby Brown sniffed the rose beads and passed them to me so I could smell their fragrant perfume.

Calgary Petroleum Products eventually hired Wong Sam, a Chinese cook, to feed its drilling crew. Youngest son Bob recalled treats the Chinaman gave the family, including sides of bacon and tinned peaches. Charlie and Uncle Bob also shot enough rabbits to augment the company's beef. Trout from Sheep Creek added variety to the menu.

Nearby, Bob and Joseph Brown helped build the wooden rig. Although imported as skilled American drillers, they worked alongside other employees and threw the rig up in just a few days. Building the wooden monster was much easier than getting the materials to the site. Timbers for the rig came by train to the closest railway station, 20 miles away at Okotoks, but from there it was all horse and wagon work. Roads were impassable during spring break-up since the dirt trails just cut across farmers' fields. In wet weather the soil turned to gumbo. Even in good weather, it took weeks to transport hundreds of beams, posts, sills, braces, and planks to the banks of Sheep Creek west of Black Diamond. While the crew built the rig, the teamsters brought in engines, boilers, drilling tools, casing, and dozens of

loads of heavy metal equipment. It all came by train from the
eastern United States.

When the Brown brothers finished building the rig they
took leftover timbers and added a few improvements to Mary's
shack. Two beams set into the ground became posts for her washing line—a length of drilling cable. She cleaned it with a rag each
wash day before hanging laundry out to dry. Other scraps of timber became a swingset for the children.

Children avoided the rig. Although the men were lax about
safety issues in these days before hardhats, a rig under construction
was no place for a kid. Besides, the men were rough. Bobby recalled that his father was not much of a drinker, but loved "rough
language." Martin Hovis and Fred Vance were other drillers. And
then there was H.A. Thompson. He earned his nickname by bet-
ting five dollars that no one could kick him off his feet. Old "Hard
Ass" never had to pay up.

The kids were busy with their own escapades. Mary tried to
tie them to the table for some lessons in reading and writing, but
their attention wandered. There was no local school. Bob recalls
a lack of store-bought toys, although his sister Josephine had a
small doll. Mostly, the kids played in the woods and caught gar-
ter snakes and water snakes along the banks of the creek. While
his brother dug the ditch for the waterline, Bob chased little animals. Fishing was popular too, and older brother Charlie used a
willow stick as a pole, a piece of string as line, and a hook to catch
trout. Supper at the Brown's often included pan-fried trout.

Holidays were much like any other day. Bob Brown re-
members Christmas as a day without much celebration. When
he awoke he found a stocking, hung on a pole. Inside were an
orange and a walnut, simple Christmas presents for the children
of a family far from home.

Life at Dingman No. 1 quickly fell into a routine. Men worked 12-hour days, seven days a week, year round. They bunked in a shack near the rig. Waste from the shacks and the rig went over the bank, into Sheep Creek, since the rig had no sump—a pit for drilling waste. There was more brush around the rig in those days so men knocked over deadfall for firewood or pulled wood up from the spring flood piles along the riverbank.

All in all, life at Dingman No. 1 was simple and mundane, boring, even, until the afternoon of May 14, 1914, when the drillers hit production at 2,718 feet and crude oil rushed up the casing and made a small geyser 15 to 20 feet above the drilling floor.

Alberta's oil industry began that day. Calgary newspapers went wild, and investors, speculators, and anyone else with a car or truck rushed over from Calgary to see the oilwell on Sheep Creek. Little Bobby Brown's playground filled with shiny cars and

Brown family home at Turner Valley, 1912-14. (Glenbow Archives, NA-5535-9)

fancily dressed people. Even the Duke and Duchess of Connaught visited the site. Dingman processed the wet gas with a system of expansion and compression chambers, distilling liquid from the gas. Many visitors filled their tanks with the clear gasoline from the well and drove home fuelled by Alberta's newest resource. Others took home a souvenir in a glass jar or bottle.

But for Bobby Brown, Turner Valley was just another chapter in the story of life as an oilman's son. The Browns packed up and moved on to California, where the men drilled more oilwells before the drilling rigs called them to far-away Alaska where they helped on discovery wells from 1919 to 1921. Canada was just a distant memory for the itinerant oil family, but they helped put western Canada on the map as a petroleum province.

Early Exploration and Investment

The lure of oil is hard to understand, in a way. Coal is hard, shiny, easy to hold in your hand, and a good source of fuel in a stove or steam engine. Gold, silver, copper and other minerals all have obvious value and make fine jewellery or fancy ornaments. Oil is different. It is sticky, tarry, a goopy liquid, and stinks. Unrefined, it burns dirty and smelly. It is explosive, dangerous, even deadly.

Life before oil was not perfect. A century after petroleum became part of everyday life, it is easy to be romantic about earlier times. Most western Canadians lived on the land and worked hard to exist. Agriculture was an unpredictable occupation because a hailstorm, drought, or plant disease could ruin a crop and devastate the family income for the year. Markets were far away too, making it tough to get a good price for grain. Those not dependent on farm income often worked in lumber camps, on railway construction crews, in underground mines, or other forms of hard labour. They lived in small shacks, with wood and coal for heat. Cutting enough wood to last through the long Canadian winter took a month or longer. Few people had running water and everyone had an outhouse in the backyard. Horses and wagons were the only transportation, or you could walk. Trains served major centres, but most Canadians lived far from the tracks. Candles and lanterns supplied light. Conveniences like electricity, telephones, water and sewer, natural gas heat, cars, radios and television had not arrived.

Western Canadians knew about oil and gas for centuries. Native peoples used it to pitch their bark canoes and as ointment for open wounds. It its raw state, it burns poorly, so Natives did not use it as fuel. The first explorers noticed it too, jotting down references in their journals to seepages along riverbanks. The tar sands stretched along the Athabasca River for miles. In some spots, smoke rose from slowly burning soil. In other places natural gas percolated up through the water in ponds or along creekbeds. Such was the case along Sheep Creek. Natives avoided drinking the water and horses moved upstream to quench their thirst. Early whites asked the Natives to take them to anything that smelled like kerosene, hoping to find minerals.

The Turner Valley oilfield lay in the middle of southern Alberta's ranching country, nuzzled against its western flank by the Rocky Mountain foothills. Ranchers arrived in this area in the 1860s. After the last buffalo disappeared, ranchers saw an opportunity to graze cattle on the endless prairie. No fences divided the land, and only natural boundaries such as rivers, mountains, and forests limited the range. Cattle fed on the open range for months. Roundups gathered the herd, and the cowboys separated their animals from the bawling mass of cows and calves and trailed them to their respective ranches. There they branded the calves and turned them out to pasture. The cowboys trailed animals to stockyards and loaded them on trains to central Canada and the United States. Many cattle boarded ship for Europe.

But the Canadian west was not empty in the days before the large ranches filled the government maps. Native people roamed the land, following an annual round of activities. Hunting buffalo by driving them over buffalo jumps in the earlier days and from horseback in more recent times, they lived off the bounty nature provided. As the buffalo disappeared, the Natives turned to other sources of game including deer, elk, and moose. They moved from the prairies to the foothills following animals and berries, spending winters in favourite sheltered valleys where frequent chinook winds moderated the cold.

When the railway arrived, nomadic ways ended and the Canadian government forced Canada's First Nations peoples onto reserves. Often, the land they received from the federal government in Ottawa was marginal for agriculture, and most Natives were not interested in raising crops. Many became cowboys or took jobs building fences when ranchers and settlers began carving up the country along section lines.

Coal Helps Find the Oil

Until the 1900s, neither Natives nor whites new much about the valuable oil and natural gas that lay beneath the surface in the western foothills. Coal was the first underground resource used by ranchers and settlers in this area. Individuals sank shafts into the riverbank and shovelled fuel for their stoves and heaters. Harry Denning, Sr. and Joe Buntz opened the first Sheep Creek coal mine in early 1888 just west of Turner Valley. The next commercial coal mine opened in 1899, northwest of the Black

Moving oilfield equipment across Sheep Creek. (Glenbow Archives, NA-2570-8)

Diamond bridge. Addison McPherson and J.I. Cooper mined 400 tons of coal that year and expanded production with six men to 650 tons annually by 1914. They sold coal as far downstream as Okotoks. A mine at the headwaters of Sheep Creek started extracting coal in the early 1900s, and ranching mogul Pat Burns bought into the company just before the First World War. Burns incorporated The Calgary and Southern Railway to transport the coal to Calgary in 1918, but Turner Valley's second oil boom in the mid-1920s ended the coal mining venture. The company graded trackbed but never laid rails because natural gas pipelines to customers largely eliminated the coal market.

Coal from the Sheep Creek mines fuelled the boilers at the discovery well in 1913 and 1914, but also indirectly contributed to oilfield development. A rancher and horsebreaker hauled Sheep Creek coal to the Okotoks electrical generation plant. Moving to Alberta from Ontario in 1905, William S. Herron bought a 960-acre property near Okotoks. He often went up Sheep Creek for coal, passing through Black Diamond, a mail distribution point for the locals by 1907. In early 1911, he collected a gas sample from the banks of Sheep Creek and sent it off for analysis. Based on his findings, Herron bought Michael Stoos' farm on the creek, where the Turner Valley Gas Plant sits today.

Local Investors Reap Rewards

Herron then set out to attract investors, and in January 1913, Calgary Petroleum Products began drilling its first well. Archibald W. Dingman, an Ontario oilman with American oilfield experience, was in charge of drilling. Lawyers James A. Lougheed and R.B. Bennett joined the company as did A.E. Cross, a famous rancher. Real estate developers also invested in CPP, as did many others in the heady boom-time economy just before the Great War.

Drilling began on January 25, 1913, with an 82-foot-high cable-tool rig powered by a coal-fuelled steam engine. The well hit gas pockets many times as the 20-inch bit cut into the soil and rock. At the 467-foot level gas flowed in a large enough quantity to replace coal as fuel for the steam boiler. The well hit gas again at the 877, 1,205, 1,235, and 1,260 foot levels. At 1,536 feet below the surface oil began to appear along with the gas. Late on Thursday afternoon, May 14, 1914, drillers hit flowing oil at 2,718 feet and crude oil rushed up the 8 1/4-inch bottom casing and made a small geyser 15 to 20 feet above the drilling floor.

William Pearce, Ottawa's eyes and ears on developments in the Canadian west from 1869 to 1904, provided the federal government with incredible detail on the life of the Canadian west in the early years of the century. Information about railways, irrigation, coal mining, and many other aspects of the development appear in his firsthand reports. The day after the Dingman discovery he filed a report with his superiors.

MEMORANDUM
Re: Oil at Calgary Petroleum Product Company's

Well, commonly known as The Dingman Well.

The well is 2,718 feet in depth. For upwards of the last 300 feet the drill has gone through a hard, compact, sandstone, barren of oil or gas. However, immediately above this sandstone there was a considerable flow of heavy wet gas. Yesterday afternoon several thin, small, gas bearing strata were encountered, and at 5:30 P.M. a heavy flow of gas was met with. Drilling then ceased, the bailer was run down and brought up considerable oil. Operations ceased. The Driller states that at 8 o'clock this morning there was 1,500 feet of oil in the hole. That, after allowing for the gas, equals 2,500 Imperial gallons of oil. (Please check, allowing 80% of the mixture as oil, 20% gas).

They are baling and filling all receptacles that will hold the fluid, but will soon run short of storage. The fluid is gasoline, 64.5 Beaume.

Just when the last oil- and gas-bearing sands were met with the sandstone assumed a much coarser grain. It is not yet known how many feet of that gas- and oil-bearing strata there may be. Some maintain that this is in the Dakotas, others claim that the probability is that the Benton is not yet reached.

More than 500 companies sprang into being in the next few days, as quickly as Calgary printers could design and print stock certificates. Most companies had no land or any intention of drilling: their business plan was to milk the public for as much money as the gullible speculators would surrender in return for worthless shares in bogus companies. Thousands of share certificates worth over a million dollars eventually wallpapered southern Alberta outhouses.

Bob Edwards reviewed the merits of these stock offerings with his usual wit in the May 23, 1914, issue of the *Calgary Eye Opener*:

> We draw particular attention to the beautiful raft of oil ads in this issue. You must really excuse us for subordinating the reading matter to advertisements just this once. It is our only chance out of this oil delirium. Of one thing you can be sure—every oil ad you see in this paper is that of a good sound company. The men behind each company advertised here are responsible Calgary businessmen, well known to everybody. No wildcatters are allowed to wander in these columns.

Small town cops kept their eyes peeled for big city speculators and handled them appropriately. The *Calgary Daily Herald* reported an incident on May 25, 1914:

Oil brokers locked up by village cops
Amusing happenings in connection with the local excitement
Cooped up in pound with stray animals
Manager of company persuaded constable to let them go

Some amusing things are bound to happen in a rush such as Calgary is now experiencing over the oil excitement, and the managers of one prominent company had a good laugh Saturday over the predicament that some of their salesmen found themselves in when they tried to sell stock in a few of the rural villages south of Calgary. It appears that a number of village constables have their tin stars all polished up just awaiting the arrival of the "city slickers," and when the stock-salesmen put in an appearance, the constables saw visions of immediate glory and reward. The unfortunate salesmen were grabbed in one village by a typical constable with a huge star and chin whiskers, and carted off to the village pound, where they were cooped up with sundry stray horses, pigs, and other unclaimed animals.

An urgent message to Calgary brought the manager of the prominent company down on the first train, breathing indignation.

"What are these men locked up for?" was the first question fired at the village limb of the law who was calmly sunning himself in front of the general store.

"I reckon you'd call it unscrupulous dealing in oil stocks," replied the worthy constable, "and they're going to stay locked up, too."

There was a great deal of argument on the subject, and after the manager had painted the future of the Calgary oil fields in glowing colours and assured the constable that the salesmen had no designs on the village bank, the unlucky men were let out of the pound. They are still combing straw out of their hair.

And so the oil stock salesmen continued on their way.

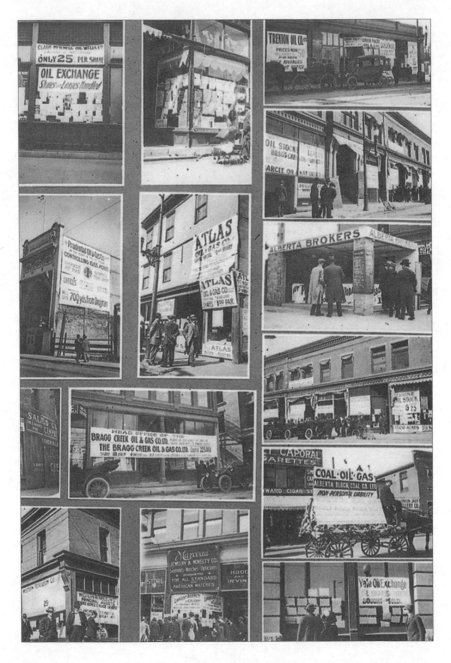

Calgary stock certificate sales, 1914. (Provincial Archives of Alberta, P1306)

The first Turner Valley boom went bust almost as quickly as it boomed, but luckily, it did not set an example for those that followed. The 1924 discovery at the Royalite No. 4 well at the north end of the town of Turner Valley started a boom that lasted until the early 1930s. When oil gushed from the ground in 1936 at the south end of the oilfield, the subsequent boom lasted until after the Second World War and set Canadian oil production records.

Imperial Oil became a major player in this oilfield after 1920. As a subsidiary of Standard Oil of New Jersey, Imperial kept its eye on every corner of Canada for its American parent. Long before pipelines connected Canadian oilfields with American customers, Standard and Imperial thought of North America as a single continental market. In its desire to dominate and control the industry, Standard did everything in its power to find oil. When, as in the case of Turner Valley, someone else found the resource, Standard tried to buy into the oilfield as quickly as possible. Herron's Calgary Petroleum Products fought the American takeover valiantly until the gas plant burned to the ground in 1920. The uninsured loss forced Herron and his partners to sell to Imperial and take a minority share in the new company, Royalite.

Imperial's new oil company wasted no time searching for oil. It also bought up competitors and quickly became the dominant company in the oilfield. Royalite No. 4's discovery in 1924 prompted more companies to drill in the oilfield. By the end of 1926, 34 companies were drilling although the Imperial Oil subsidiary was the busiest. Royalite and its sister companies were producing from five wells, had 17 rigs busy drilling around the clock and had another 36 wells ready to drill. Besides creating companies, Imperial launched a vigorous take-over program. By the mid-1930s, it held controlling interest in at least 26 Turner Valley oil companies.

The Transportation Problem

From a central camp in the town of Turner Valley, Royalite workers negotiated roads to the rigs and other field locations daily. Compared to nicely graded and paved highways throughout the area today, the roads in the 1920s were horrible and they remained a major problem throughout the first half of the century. The drive to Turner Valley from Calgary takes about one hour today on a paved road, but in the 1920s it was often a two-day ordeal from Okotoks to the oilfield. As a result, a halfway house sprang up and operated a booming business for many years. The trail across the prairie was not graded. It merely cut across open ground. In places there were turnouts so trucks could pass on the single track. In winter the route changed to avoid snowdrifts. Even when the county finally established a formal road, it jogged at farm boundaries, dipped through coulees and held tight to perilous rock ledges as it wound its way to the oilfield.

But the quickly expanding oilfield made transportation a must. Try as they might, the oil companies could not interest the CPR in putting a track to Turner Valley because the railway did not believe the expense would be warranted. Each trucking contractor was left to his own devices. No individuals cared to pay for improvements to a road that others would use for free. Companies were similarly hesitant to improve the trails. The government also refused, claiming that the oil companies should take care of their own transportation problems.

As a result, oilfield people found themselves trapped for long periods each year. Water turned the soil to gumbo, making travel impossible during spring break-up, after each rainstorm, when snow melted on unfrozen ground and whenever chinooks warmed the ground in winter. Gravel helped provide a reasonable surface, but the problem often went much deeper. An unstable base meant heavy loads quickly sank through the gravel surface and bogged down in underlying muck.

Most companies had a fleet of trucks, and contractors worked overtime hauling in supplies from Okotoks. Trucks sank to their axles in mud when road conditions were anything but perfect. As a result, caterpillar tractors normally used for construction projects became the only way to move equipment and supplies. They sometimes served as tow trucks, pulling flatbed trucks and trailers out of mud holes. The cats also pulled heavily loaded athey wagons—trailers with caterpillar tracks underneath to provide a light footprint on the soft ground. Even still, there were problems. Roy Fleiger recalled: "I remember seeing a big D-8 cat pulling one of the athey wagons loaded with 10- or 12-inch well casing up the hill between the company office and the bank corner. The road didn't look too bad before that load hit it but it couldn't stand up under that great weight and the load slowly sank down until the top of the wagon treads were level with the road. The cat driver unhooked the cat from the wagon, hooked the winch line onto the wagon tongue, drove the cat up the hill letting the winch line run out until he got up over the hill. He then put the winch in gear and gradually 'bulled' the load, not over the road but through it until it hit more solid ground. There seemed to be a spring under the road so that load just plowed its way through and the hole left behind had to be filled with several loads of rock." Rocks, not gravel, created the base for the road through this well-travelled spot.

Royalite gradually improved the roads around the Turner

Valley townsite area, its area of operations in the late 1920s. With caterpillars, graders, trucks, and other heavy machinery, it began creating a network of all-weather roads near the gas plant. But there were also times when even Royalite's equipment could not get through. For these occasions, and there were many, the company kept several horses. A tent served as a barn, complete with stalls, mangers, and even a full-time employee to take care of the mounts. According to Roy Fleiger: "One of these horses we called Angus because he was the horse Angus Sutherland, one of the old cable-tool men, used to ride. This horse was a freak. He certainly didn't look at all like a running horse but looked like he should be hitched to a plow. But that pony could get into high gear on a first jump like a quarter horse and run like a scalded cat."

The roads did not really improve much until after the last boom went bust. Florence Denning lived just south of the Turner Valley townsite and recalled the roads as constantly dusty and very bumpy when dry. In the spring the routes were a muddy, watery mess. At one point the Dennings had two cars, one on each side of the worst set of mudholes north of town. Locals improved the road with gravel hauled directly from the river. They filled larger sinkholes with large, rough rocks and then built up the surface with gravel. Highway 22 north from Turner Valley was an impassable quagmire every spring until 1955, when the municipality rebuilt it as a nice wide gravel road. When pavement arrived in 1966, the road narrowed again.

South End Exploration Hits Paydirt

Turner Valley boomed in the second half of the 1930s. From a quiet, depressed community of perhaps a thousand people in a few small settlements, the oilfield blossomed almost overnight

Oil blowing through rig, Turner Valley, 1930s. (Glenbow Archives, NA-2335-2)

into a very busy place. Thousands of people flocked to the valley, swelling its population to over 7,000. Hundreds of drilling rigs, pipeline crews, truckers, and workmen invaded the foothills oilfield after crude oil greeted the drill at the south end. The gas discoveries in 1914 and 1924 were just teasers compared to the excitement that followed the crude oil discovery in the summer of 1936.

Hints of oil were there from the beginning. Royalite No. 4 in 1924 proved that the 1914 find was just a minor trap and that deeper drilling tapped richer deposits, including more oil. By 1930, the big runaway well had produced over a million barrels of gasoline and more than 4 billion cubic feet of gas. Then it faltered. Production dropped. Engineers tried to revive the well but gave up in 1934, when they cemented it and walked away. Elsewhere, drillers found more gas. To the north and south rigs successfully tapped more reserves, proving up the small field and extending its boundaries to make it two miles wide and eight miles long.

In 1930 the Model Oil Company drilled its first of several successful wells and suffered as a result. Traces of crude oil tainted the clear naphtha, or gasoline, lowering its market value. Geologists noticed and suggested drilling along the western edge of the oilfield, wondering if the deeper part of the tilted geological formation held oil. Finally, on June 16, 1936, a well at the south end of the oilfield, near Longview, struck crude oil and Turner Valley's third boom was on its way.

Turner Valley Royalties No. 1 marked the beginning of a new era in western Canada's petroleum industry. Crude oil was the Holy Grail for the oilmen, and Alberta has always had it to spare, but it was the challenge. By the end of September the oilfield was producing almost 10,000 barrels per day, far in excess of local needs or the distribution capabilities of regional transportation systems. When the government's fiscal year ended on March 31, 1937, the once-poor province was flush with cash. Debts were a thing of the past, and the bank-profit-bashing Social Credit government of the day had to explain its way through an embarrassing million-dollar budget surplus. In a matter of a few months one of Canada's most impoverished provinces turned its financial house around and became the pride of the country.

Without oil, Alberta would have been just another province like Saskatchewan, dependent on agriculture for its future. From less than a million barrels of oil per year in 1935—it had peaked at almost 1.4 million in 1931—Turner Valley production jumped to over 2 million barrels of oil in 1936, more than 6 million in 1938, past 8 million in 1940, and to nearly 10 million barrels per year at its historic high during the Second World War. Most of the nearly 120 million barrels of oil that came out of the Turner Valley field between 1924 and 1960 resulted from the oil discovered in 1936.

Drilling Conditions and Labour Problems

Oil does not erupt unbidden from the ground, at least not in Alberta. Hard work goes into coaxing petroleum to leave its underground reservoirs and come to the surface. The first oil wells in North America were exactly that, oil wells, dug by hand much like water wells. Then came springpole rigs, in which a bent pole jigged a metal bit up and down in a hole, drilling by pounding the bit into the earth.

The first rigs in the Canadian West were not much more evolved than springpoles. Cable-tool drilling systems relied on the same basic principle but applied it on a grander scale. Rig builders first constructed a massive wooden rig. First, days of pick and shovel work roughed out a hole for a 8 x 10-foot cellar and about as deep. Valves and other equipment eventually found a home in this hole. Above the cellar men built the foundation for the rig with massive timbers. Boards on it made a floor upon which they built everything else. Then plank by plank, the rig rose into the sky above the cellar. Twenty feet square at the bottom, the wooden rig tapered 85 feet into the air where it was only five feet square.

The men who built the rig had to be strong and not fear heights. With an apron full of spikes and a heavy hammer, they worked their way up. The corners of the rig were not single beams, but a series of planks nailed together at right angles. Horizontal boards or girts held the corners stable every eight feet and diagonals called sway braces provided more rigidity. Rig builders worked in pairs, and men on the ground passed up timbers or tied them to ropes so the builders could yank them up. Standing on a 2 x 12-inch girt, each man added planks above him in the corners of the rig, positioning them temporarily with 5-inch spikes and finishing the job as the rig rose. Then the partners threw another girt overhead and drove spikes through it into the legs of the rig. Further up the rig they used 1 x 12-inch girt material, making it easier to lift but providing an even narrower walkway. The builders topped the rig off with a crown block, a series of pulley-wheels called sheaves. Three cables ran through these pulleys: the drilling line for lifting and dropping the bit that bashed through the rock, the sand line for running a bailer down to bring out the cuttings mixed with water, and the casing line to install the steel pipe that served as a casing or sleeve in the hole and kept the sides of the hole from caving in. Cables from the top of the rig ran out in all four directions and anchored the wooden tower against stiff foothills winds.

Building the rig was just the beginning. Beside it sat the engine house connected with a walkway to the rig. Various other shacks and sheds held machinery and there was a lunch room and an outhouse. Every building needed solid walls and a watertight roof. Compared to today's rotary rigs that can drill a well in a few days or weeks, cable-tool outfits were terribly slow. They often took years to reach oil-bearing levels. So the old rigs had to protect the drillers and their helpers from rain, sleet, snow, and howling blizzards, day and night, for hundreds of days.

Drilling With Cable Tools

Life on the rig floor was dull, not glamorous. Three men worked each shift: a driller, a tool-dresser, and a fireman. In the engine house, the fireman stoked the 40-horsepower steam boiler with wood or coal to keep the boiler hot and produce steam. Natural gas served as fuel after the well hit a gas flow, but for the first months the fireman sweated as he shovelled coal or threw lengths of cordwood into the boiler. He also made sure the thirsty boiler never ran out of water. With an eye on the pressure gauge, the fireman kept the steam pressure steady for the driller.

Nearby, the tool-dresser stoked a hot fire of coking coal burning in a little furnace. His job was to physically re-form the face of the drilling tools with nothing more complicated than heat and a hammer. His work was that of a blacksmith, with a twist. Drilling bits were up to 24 inches across, massive, cylindrical tools that weighed as much as a ton. Wedge-shaped across the face, they cut rock and bashed their way into the earth under their own momentum. Although made of toughened steel, they lost their cutting edge and spread with each impact. The tool-dresser regularly repaired these battered instruments. After heating the bit in a hot fire, he hoisted it onto a platform and beat it back into rough shape with hammers, finishing off the job with chisels and files.

The fireman and tool-dresser also helped the driller as

Drillers Martin Hovis and Joseph Brown at Dingman Discovery Well, 1914. (Provincial Archives of Alberta, P1303)

required. From his position at the base of the rig, the driller directed the operations. With a telegraph wheel and cord he controlled a valve at the far end of the rig that released steam into the piston. A 90-foot-long stitched rubber belt transferred power from the flywheel to the band wheel which in turn moved the pitman arm at one end of the walking beam. The string of tools hung from the other end of the walking beam and moved up and down in the hole when drilling. With his hand on the drilling cable, the driller felt the action of the bit. If the cable was slack, it was not lifting the tool from the bottom of the hole; if it was too tight, it was not hitting the bottom. The driller adjusted a turnbuckle on the drilling cable to keep the tension balanced and rotated a bar on the temper screw to keep the bit rotating and cutting a true hole. After drilling a few feet, the driller pulled the string of tools from the hole and set it to one side on the derrick floor. He then dumped a barrel of water into the hole and lowered a bailer with the sand reel, using steam power and a series of mechanical brakes to operate the winches and pulleys. The bailer was a hollow piece of pipe with a one-way watertight valve at one end. The valve activated when it hit the bottom of the hole, opening and allowing the muddy water and cuttings to flow up into its hollow centre. The driller pulled it out of the well and dropped it into the dump box, a chute that sent the drilling waste through the rig floor and down the cutbank into Sheep Creek. The driller sometimes took rock samples from the slurry as it spilled into the dump box. Saved in small cotton bags, they became part of the drilling log. Part geologist, carpenter, manager, mechanic and dowser, the driller was responsible for everything that happened at the well during his shift.

Likely as not, something went wrong. Men failed to show for work or arrived drunk, the manila drilling line broke in the well and left the tools hundreds of feet below the surface, the coal delivery man failed to show up with fuel for the boiler, or the investors ran out of money and the crew got an unexpected holiday, unpaid.

Central Turner Valley Discovery Wells – 1914 and 1924

The first Turner Valley discovery well suffered through most of these problems. Money was not hard to get, though, with nearby Calgary in the midst of a real estate speculation boom. As fast as companies printed stock, Calgarians poured their savings and speculation profits into Turner Valley wells. As a result, Herron and Dingman had little trouble finding money to pay the men who drilled Calgary Petroleum Products No. 1.

When the oil came in on May 14, 1914, it a rush on oil industry stock for a few months, and it allowed the independent oil company to build a small refinery. Once the First World War broke out, drilling continued slowly in the new oilfield. By 1920, crews had spudded in 19 wells, seven of which they abandoned. Four were still drilling, six were successful oil wells and two produced only gas. The best well produced 40 barrels of oil per day, but 10 barrels was average. It took about two years to drill a well to the 3,500 foot level and each well cost more than $50,000.

The oilfield stumbled along as a minor player until 1924, when another discovery well created the second Turner Valley boom. The early 1920s were quiet times in southwestern Alberta, with few folk noticing the occasional well that drilled for oil. Milt Ward was known far and wide throughout southern Alberta as a rancher from near the small community of Arrowwood. He became a fixture at most every auction, buying up collectibles to fill his huge storage barn. But Milt also remembered the early days of the Turner Valley oilfield. Each spring he ran a herd of cattle to leased land at the headwaters of Sheep Creek. Several times during summer he returned to check the herd, stopping in each time to see how the drillers were doing on Royalite No. 4. Starting in September, 1922, Sid Bagley and Clarence Snyder worked long shifts, 12 hours at a time, operating the cable-tool rig as it bashed its way down through more than 3,000 feet of rock. Mostly it was monotonous work and they were glad to visit with the rancher. They discussed the weather, cattle prices, road conditions, anything to pass the long hours. Milt listened as they explained the simple drilling process, watched with wonder as the tool-dresser swung his monstrous sledge hammer against a red-hot bit to reshape and sharpen it to cut into the rock again. They even let him put his hand on the drilling cable as it jerked up and down in the well, lifting and dropping the heavy bit at the bottom of the hole.

Seasons passed and still Bagley and Snyder worked two shifts each day, without incident. Finally, in early November 1923 the well hit gas at the 2,871 foot level, flowing about 7 million cubic feet of gas per day. Royalite immediately diverted the sweet gas to its pipeline to Calgary. Drilling continued in the spring, trying to push through the limestone rock, down 3,450 feet. Then came Tronson Draper, a new superintendent from Toronto. He told the men to stop drilling. Field Manager Sam Coultis disagreed, pointing out that no other company was likely to break through the limestone to see what it held. On into the fall the rig drilled, slowly deepening the hole. As the drillers worked through the long night of October 12, 1924, the dreaded event happened: the tools got stuck. Down 3,740 feet into the hole, the tools jammed. It did no good to pull on them, yank on them, loosen the cable, curse at them, or drop things down on them—they were stuck. So the men began a "fishing" operation. With various hooks, jams, and other tools, they tried to release the drilling string. Failure would be embarrassing and expensive and would mean leaving the tools in the hole and starting again nearby. Drillers tried every trick in the book before abandoning an uncompleted well. No driller wanted the reputation for leaving tools in the ground.

Then, with a rush, natural gas liquids began screaming out of the well. Temperature at the wellhead dropped to -20°F. The mighty flow jarred the tools loose, only to jam them together again further up the well, nearly stopping the gas flow of 21 million cubic feet of gas and 300 barrels of gasoline per day. Then the drilling cable snapped and fell in a lump on top of the useless tools. During this lull in the action, the drillers filled the well with water as protection against another blow-out and hooked the cable with fishing tools. Then the well erupted again, blowing water everywhere and sending rock chips flying out of the well which cut the second drilling cable, leaving two sets of tools and two cables in the hole.

The Royalite crew attached a large, 3,000-pound valve to the well casing and closed off the flow. Pressure grew, exceeding 1,150 pounds per square inch in just a few minutes. Then the valve began to rise inside the wooden derrick, pushed skyward atop 94 tons of 8¼-inch casing. When the valve reached the top of the cable-tool rig, the casing separated far below the surface and the valve and largest string of casing settled back into the earth. Gas leaked around the valve, up around the casing and even percolated up through the ground around the well. And this gas stank of bad eggs—a sure sign of deadly hydrogen sulphide in the gas.

Sour Gas and Hell's Half Acre

The history of the petroleum industry in Turner Valley changed that day when Royalite No. 4 penetrated the limestone gas cap and began producing sour gas. Before October 1924, the oilfield's sweet gas had an immediate market in Calgary and other

Burning seepage at Columbia Oil Number One Well, 1936. (Provincial Archives of Alberta, P8568)

southern Alberta communities. After October 1924, producing companies had to process Turner Valley gas and scrub out the noxious hydrogen sulphide. This was all in the quest for crude oil which went unrewarded for another dozen years.

A week after the initial discovery, on October 19, 1924, all hell broke loose. Bert Flathers was working on the Royalite No. 4 well that day, stacking casing pipe. "At noon everyone went to the cookhouse, down by the plant, for dinner. While we were eating we heard an explosion. We all ran outside to look and the gas pressure had blown the tools and everything through the top of the derrick. We watched as a big silver cloud of gas moved across the field. When it reached the Dalhousie boilers it ignited. There was a big flash and No. 4 was on fire. It was just lucky that we were all at dinner so no one was hurt." From the bedroom of his home on a nearby hill, a nine-year-old boy named Don watched as the events of that Sunday made history: "I seen the ball of fire go from the stack on the boiler and go through the air and set the gas on fire." A few minutes later the wooden rig was ashes, the metal parts twisted industrial waste. Don's father, Sam Coultis, was manager of the simple Royalite gas plant beside the Dingman No. 1 discovery well, would have to find something profitable to do with the sour gas.

But first Royalite had to deal with a massive blow-out. A wild well is an incredible monster to behold, complete with screaming gas, billowing flames, intense heat, and violently shaking ground. It is like nothing else in nature though the forces that create it are natural. Trapped far below the surface, oil and gas are subject to massive geological forces and intense compression. Gas and oil migrate from high-pressure areas, finding their way to the surface where gas dissolves into the atmosphere and the seasons wash away the oil. But where porous formations lie under impervious layers of rock, gas and oil accumulate in traps and when these are tapped into the resulting blow-outs can be spectacular.

Today, geologists and geophysicists use their theories, drilling information, and seismic records to find these pockets of hydrocarbons, but in the early days the drillers based their drilling decisions on surface seepages, and on luck. Finding oil is tricky business. Royalite's decision to drill into the Madison limestone took it to greater depths than other western Canadian oilwells. The sour gas blow-out that shrieked into life in October 1924, was typical of the other kind of luck that often greets the drill bit: bad luck. In remote locations drillers sometimes walk away from wild wells and let them blow themselves out with time, sometimes decades later. But Royalite No. 4 was near Calgary and the gas pocket it discovered was both deadly and potentially valuable. Besides, once the gas from the well caught on fire, it made a pillar of flame that reached far into the sky. Tourists and locals began visiting the wild well and light from it was visible throughout the night sky for hundreds of miles around southern Alberta. The blow-out was famous.

But it embarrassed Royalite. No one knew what to do with the well. The pressure exceeded anything the drillers had ever encountered and the hydrogen sulphide made the gas as smelly as it was deadly. So the fire burned out of control for weeks. Gas blasted out of the ground, making a large crater and sucking dirt with it into the pillar of fire. Royalite's employees scrambled to put out the fire and bring the wild well under control, but without success. Albert Smith began his oilfield career helping fight this blowout. "I had a team of horses on a slip and Harry E. Denning also had a team fastened to the same slip with about 75 feet of cable. One of us would pull the slip across and the other would pull it back filling the cellar with dirt to help put out the fire which was burning there." With horses, cables, and road-building scrapers, they filled the burning crater with soil and extinguished the burning ground. "In the meantime they kept the whole thing drenched with steam so it wouldn't re-light."

But the tall flume of gas was still ablaze. Royalite's drilling superintendent, Bill Applegate, imported two wild-well experts from Oklahoma, Richardson and Downes. They lined up seven steam boilers. On their signal, pent-up steam from the massive locomotive boilers blasted the flame, but the tower of fire refused to go out. Albert Smith recalled their next attempt: "They rigged up a steam line onto a big funnel and when we got the cellar filled and the fire out around the casing, with dirt and steam, they pulled the funnel over the hole and got the fire going through the funnel and then snatched it out."

"Snatching out" a fire hundreds of feet high was not a simple task. The only way to extinguish a blaze is to take away its source of fuel. This wild well provided its own source of gas, but the atmosphere provided the oxygen necessary to keep the flare alive. So they fought fire with fire. Charlie Stalnaker came up from Casper, Wyoming, where he worked for the International Torpedo Company. Charlie had nerves of steel and the common sense to work with liquid nitro-glycerine and its safer replacement, dynamite, for more than 50 years. When he arrived at the Canadian border, customs officials and border guards just stood aside and waved the explosives man through, tall red flags flapping at each corner of his specially equipped car or truck. At the Royalite No. 4 well Charlie loaded dynamite into a canister and attached a long cable. Everyone stood back. Charlie pulled the dangerous explosive towards the flare carefully, coordinating the timing of the burning fuse to ignite the dynamite beside the flame. As soon as the explosion robbed the spewing gas of its oxygen and extinguished the fire, steam engineers opened the valves on their boilers and blanketed the area with wet steam to prevent a spark re-igniting the well.

With the fire out, crews of workmen moved in, cemented a wellhead in place and finally brought the wild well under full control on December 9, 1925—more than seven weeks after the well became a pillar of fire. The well eventually produced more than a million barrels of naphtha—gasoline—and Royalite made more than $3 million from that well. This 1924 discovery created a second boom in the Turner Valley field that lasted until the early 1930s.

Brutal Busts

Oilpatch booms often happen overnight and the busts are often just as fast and terribly brutal. In 1930 Royalite had 26 rigs

Seismic truck, 1950. (Provincial Archives of Alberta, P3019)

working in the Turner Valley field. By Stampede week in 1931, the oilfield's major employer had just two rigs working, staffed with drilling supervisors in order to keep them employed. Even these skilled men lost their jobs that fall. Ralph Steen recalled his first oilfield job, working as the water boy on a ditching crew. He carried a large bucket of water from a spring to the crew and served it to them in Dixie cups. The ditch was up the hill across the river from the plant, across from the Royalite No. 2 flare. The men dug the trench seven feet deep with picks and shovels. They started on June 5, 1930, and by July 1, 1930, they were all laid off. In early 1932, Royalite's corporate parent, Imperial Oil, reported that it aided 115 Turner Valley families with 576 food hampers for a cost of $5,328.17, an expense it considered an emergency measure. Imperial expected the government to take over relief administration soon.

Bob Danforth was a skilled farmer, trucker, and heavy equipment operator working in the late 1920s for a company that served the oilfield. His daughter, Erma Brown, recalled that his skills did not prepare him for the downturn. "During the '30s when jobs were few and far between, each morning Bob took his lunch and walked to Turner Valley in hopes there would be a job available that day. He had to be there before seven o'clock in the morning, and almost always there was no job, or the bosses just picked a few men, and the rest were left to another time. Then he would have to walk the three miles home."

American Labour Problem

Added to the unemployment in the early 1930s was the problem of American workers. Although they brought new skills and technology, the Americans stole jobs from Canadians. Many American drilling crews arrived as a team. They came to drill, not to create work for Canadians. But one of these Americans, a real "old reprobate" as one oldtimer recalled, came with a reputation and personality so much bigger than life that it was hard not to like him.

Pat and Lorraine Tourond could talk for hours about old John Norman. Old "Buckethead" Norman was one of the best drillers to ever work rotary rigs in Turner Valley. He also knew how to play poker, and lose all his money, in the back of the truck while driving to work. John spoke with a deep southern drawl. He came into the world in the middle of the night in 1904 in Lindsay, Oklahoma, on the Washita River. His grandmother said he was born under an apple tree because "It was too hot to have a baby in the house."

By his mid-twenties, John was in the Turner Valley field,

drilling wells at Hartell for Boller, Sherman and Boller Co. A week after meeting Frances Trahan, he married her in High River. His wedding proposal: "Get yer bonnet on gal, we'uns is goin' to tie the knot." That took 15 minutes. John gave the priest ten dollars, a dollar less than he paid for the ring. "Then in 1931, we had us a snotty nosed gal, and we named her Yvonne Betty, wanted a boy, but had to take what the Lord gives."

Buckethead was young when he arrived in Canada and he worked his way up through every job on the rig until he was a top driller. Sketchy accounts of his early days implied that he could more than take care of himself and was perhaps on the run from the law. He claimed the prison warden had a mean dog, named Old Blue. The warden said that no one could escape due to the meanness of the dog. "Well, I escaped," he said, "and Old Blue went along with me."

He got his nickname with the same bravado. Pat Tourond recalled the incident. "He was fishing in Hector's Dam out by Hartell, so John took his boat fishing out there and the motor come off of the boat, slipped down to the bottom of the lake. When he come up to work, at the drilling rig, the driller said 'Well John, if you put a bucket over your head and go down in the water, the air stays in the bucket.' So he got one of the rough-necks, the cat-head man by the name of Bennett, to row the boat for him. So over the edge John went to get his motor. Well, he didn't come up, and he didn't come up so the guy thought 'I'm getting pretty worried, I better go get the RCMP to drag this damn lake.' Lo and behold, he was just getting ready to go and here John walked out on the shore. In his hand he had the cutting bar off a mowing machine. So he says 'When I went down for that motor, I saw this and I thought I better get the cuttin' bar off of it in case somebody got tangled in it.' I don't know how long he was down there, but the guy got worried. The name always stuck on him, Buckethead Norman. There was nothing he wouldn't attempt."

Norman was a bold roughneck. He could climb the rig like a monkey and he liked jokes. He learned to work the derrick so the company laid off the derrick man. A few weeks later Norman got a letter: "Come back and work derrick," it said, "the monkey's drilling."

He was one of the best drillers in the business. He often played the fool, calling his superiors "Mister Bossman," but, a quick study, he was willing to try anything. Once, while running casing into a well under great pressure, John made a mistake and the toolpush asked, "John, didn't you ever run casing before?" Came the reply: "This rig and one more will be two, Mister Boss." And he know how to drink. An oilman once made the mistake of handing him an open bottle of booze. "I always like my drink off the bottom," he said, after draining the contents. He liked his home brew too: "That really made our eyes think they were spring loaded."

When times were tough in the early 1930s, he apparently stole a joint of drill stem, weighing about six hundred pounds, carried it off and sold it for cash. He never went on welfare, choosing to vary his diet until the good times returned. "Our vittles were kind of different for a couple of years or so. We ate gopher, the meat was stronger, but if you were hungry, you closed your eyes and thought of something else, it sure filled the spot. Now, porkypine was beautiful meat. Pigeon, fish, dandelion leaves, skunk cabbage, wild onions, and when available, flour to make bannock. Yep, sure was different than now days."

Although he loved to entertain company, he was often out fly-fishing on the river. He loved wrestling too, listening to radio broadcasts of the big fights whenever he could. People in need could count on John, and he is on the record for saving at least six people from drowning. When Red Young's house caught fire, Norman waded into the flames, found the baby girl, threw her out the back door into the safety of an onlooker's arms and then brought out Mrs. Young. She eventually died of her burns.

When things turned around, Norman did well again. Not a believer in banks, he carried large amounts of cash on his person. He once bought a house for his daughter, so the story goes, and paid $85,000 in large bills from two fat wallets. He retired to a life of trucking, hauling water for rigs. That company lasted almost 18 years before he sold it out. After 50 years in the valley he summarized his time in western Canada's first oilfield with a few words: "Mighty fine, mighty fine."

If could have been mighty fine for Canadians too. As Irene Dyck, who began teaching school in Turner Valley in 1931, recalled, "When the Americans first came in they wouldn't even hire a Canadian as a waterboy." Canadians had the skills, too, many of them coming from Ontario's famous oilfield at Petrolia. But where American oil companies became dominant, they overlooked local laws and treated new oilfields as mere extensions of their American properties. Turner Valley was just a northern part of Texas or Oklahoma as far as Americans were concerned in the 1920s and 1930s. The Americans also saw Canadian oil as part of their birthright. They battled with Britain for control over Turner Valley oil and, when the Second World War broke out, they extended their sphere of influence to include much of the Canadian North.

In some ways, the Americans were needed; the American oilmen had experience in oilfield work and most of the equipment used in Turner Valley came from American suppliers. But the Turner Valley field was not an extension of the geological formations that held oil in the southern states. Western Canadian oilfields were plagued by sour gas, extremely high-pressure and twisted geological formations caused problems that even experienced Americans found challenging. Beginning in the 1920s, Canadian drillers, engineers and field workers solved these complex technological problems with home-grown solutions, adding to their international reputation as innovators.

The Americans flocked into the Turner Valley field, arriving in a new surge after each discovery. None stayed after the first boom, though the Royalite No. 4 discovery in 1924 attracted ongoing attention. When the drill found reserves a few miles south-east, Hartell sprang up overnight, full of Americans. The settlement was named after a local ranching and farming family. Alex and Lillian Hartell got to know the imports very well. The oilmen, mostly working for a drilling contractor named Bowler, rode on a truck from High River into Turner Valley to work. Alex said Bowler "sure woke us up. He brought us a different style of life. We found out we didn't have to sleep in the same bed every night. They were a wild bunch of Yanks." Lillian recalled that "they drank a lot. They played a lot. You never knew which one was with whose wife." And the Yanks were good ball players too.

Kay Droppo recalled the American invasion with exceptional clarity: "They were very extravagant people and fascinated us. They were Cajuns, Creole, Quadroon Indian. Some brought their wives, some brought somebody else's wife and some brought broads. The women dressed beautifully and they were beautiful women, with a drawl that kept you entertained. The men drove cars larger than our bosses did. The latest thing was white wall tires. They drank a lot of whiskey and were very congenial people and sociable. They were good for us, because we were very

Drillers Joseph Brown and Martin Hovis, 1914. (Provincial Archives of Alberta, P1840)

conservative." She thought the Americans taught the Canadians a lot about oilfield work and about life. Turner Valley people learned to drink, dance, fight, and loosen up a bit and the result was good. She thought Turner Valley people became the best in the world. "They are loyal people. Loyal to their country, loyal to their employers, loyal to each other, and loyal to themselves.

They do not shirk. They were people of necessity and were equal to the occasion. They are my people."

Jean McLeod and her husband ran a store in Turner Valley and she thought the Americans made quite an impression in the early days. "It got to be more like a little American town. If you lived here and went to someplace else, you'd notice quite a difference in the people's outlook. Things were speeded up here on account of the oil business." The Americans bought fancy things in the store.

Melvina Briggs recalled that her mother, Rose, took in washing for the American oilmen who lived in the bunkhouse. She thought the Americans were much like the others that passed through the boom town. "I can't really say they were different. I know quite a few of them skipped out in the middle of the night and left huge grocery bills and things like that. And those who rented houses, the owners sometimes didn't get their rent money. They'd be here for a few months and then gone, suddenly, but there were others who were very good, honest. Same as all people. There were the good and the bad in every bunch."

Bill McIntyre knew many Americans from the early years. He found them snobbish, not always ready to associate with Canadians. Charlie Woo said they thought of themselves "as bigger people." RCMP officer "Bus" Rivett said the Americans drove bigger cars, brought their attitudes with them and "tried to show the poor Canadians up." Bill Lockhart recalled the Americans seemed to think they were better than the Canadians. They were, as a group, "poor salesman for their own country."

James H. Gray got to know the oilpatch through his work as the editor of the *Oil and Gas Review*, a Calgary newspaper. He said they arrived in great droves when they found out that they could get drilling reservations and that after finding oil they could keep one third of it as a drilling lease. This was different from in the United States, because there the mineral rights were usually owned by the landowners, not the government.

W.O. Mitchell recalled lots of Americans coming through High River where he taught school during Turner Valley's boom period. According to him, many were on the run from the law, escaping murder charges in their home states in the far south. But as far as he was concerned, "The British were held in more distaste than ever the Americans were."

The American labour problem became a public issue in the 1920s and continued to plague the Turner Valley into the 1950s. When Ottawa passed a law in 1929 that forbade foreign "contract labour" from entering Canada, several Americans oilworkers from the American South on the way to jobs in Turner Valley were stranded in Montana. Outraged company officials lobbied Ottawa quickly and forced it to change the law. Americans then poured into the oilfield. An editorial in the *Calgary Herald* suggested Canada should welcome skilled Americans into Turner Valley but noted that unskilled American workers were entering the oilfield on tourist visas and working indefinitely, stealing jobs from unemployed Canadians. A few weeks later, a Canadian veteran with 30 years' experience in the international oilpatch told the *Herald* that Canadians were as skilled as any drillers in the world. He pointed out that since Canadians were prohibited by law from working in the American oilfields, Americans should be kept out of Turner Valley.

Americans not only worked in the oilfield, they often controlled the operations. In one case, an American driller assaulted a Canadian worker. Canadian law required steam operating engineers to shut down machinery for periodic inspection and maintenance. However, an American driller demanded total control of one drilling operation and, when the engineer attempted to obey the law and service his machinery, the American physically assaulted the Canadian engineer. The case ended up in court in 1930.

After the slow period in the early 1930s, the Turner Valley oilfield boomed once again in 1936. That year's census listed 255 Americans out of 969 men employed in Alberta's oil industry. The local Turner Valley newspaper repeatedly complained about the American labour problem and stated that Canadian nationals routinely lost jobs to Americans. It questioned the need to import Americans when Canadians could do the work. It also suggested an association for oilfield workers. The editor said the workers needed protection from outside labour, the oil companies, and the government. Only an organization familiar with the workers' needs could adequately represent their point of view. Complaints about Americans in the oilfield continued. Finally, on July 11, 1938, N.E. Tanner, Acting Minister of Trade and Industry for Alberta, wrote his boss, Deputy Minister W.D. King, and asked him to investigate the American drillers in Turner Valley.

In an attempt to control American immigration to the oilfield, the Alberta government had enjoyed a longstanding agreement with the federal government that any drillers who applied to work in the oilfield would have their immigration applications passed on to the provincial authorities for consideration. On July 21, 1938, L.J. Ricks of Calgary told his superior, M.W. Robertson of the Alberta Employment Service in Edmonton that American drilling contractors Newell and Chandler employed American drillers instead of Canadians. When drilling slowed they fired Canadians first, but those laid off refused to submit a written complaint for fear of "discrimination." Robertson investigated and found that no Americans had received permission from the

Alberta Employment Service to work in the oilfield. His final report to W.D. King showed special treatment for American drillers. Newell and Chandler, aware of immigration restrictions and the agreement between Ottawa and Edmonton, hired Calgary lawyer Eric Harvie to appeal directly to the federal Minister of Immigration in Ottawa. Harvie's actions allowed Newell and Chandler to import Americans. Robertson stated that this action contravened the existing agreement between the two levels of government and called for immediate licensing and provincial registration of all oilfield workers in an attempt to control the American labour problem.

Registration of oilfield workers took place in 1938. During the Second World War many skilled workers of all nationalities worked for the war effort, but the problem with American labour continued. As late as 1950, the local trade magazine, the *Western Oil Examiner*, still called for a limit to the number of American drillers in the Alberta oilfield.

Oilpatch Unemployment

During the 1930s, an employment agency of sorts set up shop in the Turner Valley Log Cabin Café, but there was little work to find. Unsavoury employers sometimes greeted those who landed a job. Calgary lawyer E.A. Dunbar wrote George Hoadley, the Member of the Legislative Assembly of Alberta for the area, complaining about unethical practices of oilfield companies. Some companies refused to pay their employees, he claimed. Once the province gained control over its natural resources, he recommended it include conditions in lease agreements to protect workers.

Meanwhile, the tough times intensified. Tens of thousands of Canadians could not find work. Governments could do little or nothing to help during the international economic slump, and the future looked very grim. Men rode the rails, catching boxcar rides on trains to that elusive part of Canada where they might find a job. There were no jobs, and hobo camps sprang up under railway bridges and near nuisance grounds, now called landfill sites. George de Mille remembered the unemployed sleeping by flares to stay warm. Some even built small shelters. The single men walked through the settlements looking for scraps to eat and odd jobs to do. But even the locals needed work. Before the villages themselves went bankrupt, they tried to force the unemployed to work in return for the small relief cheques. Not surprisingly, the men almost all had bad backs. One man even injured his back while doing road work and received compensation.

Individuals did the best they could. A garden helped families keep food on the table. Rick Smith spent his childhood in the south end of the oilfield and his family also relied on a garden. Most everyone grew some vegetables and guarded them with their lives. One family had a cow that sometimes got loose. Edna McKellar remembered one neighbour who took extraordinary measures: "The cow got into a garden and so Fred got up. He didn't wear any pyjamas when he went to bed, so he just jumped up and went out to chase that cow out of the garden. He was chasing it down the street towards the church and a car came around the corner and the headlights shone right on Fred and there he was without a stitch of clothes on." He turned and ran for home, but the car followed him right up the street to his house, driven by Dr. Dave Lander on a house call to Fred's address.

Families on relief fared only slightly better than single men. Maurice Edwards' father and mother received $7.50 per month to support a family. They trapped and hunted to stay alive, bringing home weasels, coyotes, and deer. The fur dealer paid 25¢ for a weasel skin, $3 for a coyote. When he got a bit older, Maurice hauled water to make money.

Maurice's career in the oilpatch showed how a creative

Rig crew member, Turner Valley. (Glenbow Archives, NA-67-113)

personality could spin wages and contract work into a regular income. In 1939, Maurice Edwards took a job as a separator man, two days per week, for $45 per month. Even when he took over the well full time for $90 per month, he was bored: "There was very little to do." He moved a 14 x 16-foot shack onto the lease and exterminated the bedbugs with 2-4-D. He also sold all the gasoline he could make for $3 per barrel to the locals, often making more from sales than from wages. With a cow, some chickens and pigs on the lease, he lived comfortably in the south end of the oilfield. On days off he also took jobs cleaning wax out of oil tanks for $50. The work only took a day, but he had to hire a helper to crank a pump outside that delivered fresh air to his mask. One helper was not too bright: he cranked the pump quickly for a while and then walked away for a smoke, leaving Maurice gasping for air inside the stuffy tank. When the government rationed gas during the Second World War, Maurice built a still from a 45-gallon oil drum. He lit a fire under a barrel full of oil and slowly cooked the brew, taking vapours off through a coil in a wooden feeding trough full of snow—he only did this in winter—and then into another barrel. This system made about 30 gallons of gasoline in 24 hours.

This oilman somehow managed to keep all his body parts with him till retirement, but not all oilfield workers were so lucky. Pat Tourond, for example, gave more than most to the work. One Sunday he and another fellow decided to work overtime, moving a house for Home Oil. Pat continued: "The winch slipped as I was lifting the block out and I left my finger right in the glove." A co-worker found the digit and tacked it up on a board at work, where it cured perfectly. "They left it a day or two there so they wrapped it up and sent it home in my lunch pail. My wife was getting ready to cut a lunch for the next day and out dropped the finger. So it didn't go over very big at home here."

Rotary Rigs Made a Difference

As drilling evolved during the mid-1930s, the search for oil went through a hybrid phase: cable tools and rotary both figured in the famous crude oil discovery at the south end. Beginning on April 17, 1934, Roy Widney drilled the first 4,500-foot-deep well at Turner Valley Royalties No. 1 with cable tools. Then money ran out. After the investors pounded on enough doors to raise more money and Imperial Oil and British American joined the project, Roy talked Bob Brown Sr. into switching over to rotary drilling.

The fast rotary rig—the basic technology still in use to-day—was more dangerous than the plodding old cable-tool outfit. The rig was steel, taller, sometimes up to 180 feet high. Early rotary rigs used steam power produced by three or more steam boilers, but by the end of the 1940s most rigs relied on natural gas or diesel power. Instead of a hole in the floor with a cable and tools jigging slowly up and down, a steel turntable rotated in the middle of the floor on the rotary rig. Bits on the bottom of a string of drill pipe cut into the earth as power rotated the turntable, literally drilling the bit into the ground. Instead of pulling the bit every few feet to bail out the cuttings like in a cable-tool outfit, the drillers only had to pull the drilling string to replace worn out bits. Various pulleys in the crown block at the top of the rig helped pull the pipe, run it back in, lower casing, and do many other heavy lifting jobs. The mud, under pressure, cooled the drilling, removed the cuttings, plastered the outside wall of the well to keep it from caving, sealed out salt or fresh water, and controlled the flow of gas or oil as necessary. In a perfect world.

In spite of drilling problems, the well made a major crude oil discovery on June 16, 1936, flowing 850 barrels of oil a day. Not only did the well prove that crude oil existed in commercial quantities in Alberta, it graphically marked the transition from the old percussive method of drilling used by the cable tools to the modern rotary technology. The *High River Times* sang the praise of the new well in an article it titled "Crude Oil Booms Turner Valley Area." Although Royalite No. 4 teased the dreams of the speculators and caused promoters to drill 180 wells by the end of 1935, the *Times* credited the discovery in the south end of the field with writing a "New Chapter" in Alberta's oil history. "With the start of the depression years in 1930, oil production declining for a time....On June 16, 1936, the new and dramatic chapter of the oil industry was opened by production of Turner Valley Royalties on the west flank. This is now regarded as a pioneer of the heavy crude oil producers. Production settled to 550 barrels daily, increased to 900 barrels by acidization with gravity of 44.9 baume."

Chapter 2

The Turner Valley Gas Plant

The Turner Valley gas plant was a central feature of the oilfield for 70 years. Its story began soon after Dingman No. 1 well found oil and gas in May 1914. Although Calgary Petroleum Products (CPP) was not the only company active in the Turner Valley field, its activities gave it a dominant position in early Alberta oilpatch history. The company spudded in a second well only 11 days after its discovery well struck oil.

Then CPP installed North America's second absorption plant on the banks of Sheep Creek. The Hope Natural Gas company, a subsidiary of Standard Oil of New Jersey, built and installed the first American absorption plant in 1913 and the unit at Turner Valley the next year. An American named Ed Fryer built this absorption plant for about $70,000, and it operated until the fire in 1920. The business of processing natural gas in Canada dates to this site.

Although Herron and Dingman launched the first natural gas processing plant in Canada, they had a serious marketing problem: they had no way to move gas to Calgary. Eugene Coste's Canadian Western Natural Gas, Light, Heat and Power Company Limited had obtained a monopoly on the natural gas market in the city of Calgary two years earlier. Coste connected the Bow Island gas field, discovered in 1909, to Calgary consumers on July 24, 1912, with a 170-mile-long, 16-inch pipeline.

CPP used some gas for power and heating but flared most of it as a by-product of the refining process. Calgary customers, served by a gas monopoly that kept increasing it rates and ran short of gas in the cold winter months, noticed the bright glow in the southwestern sky as Turner Valley flares burned millions of cubic feet of valuable gas each day. The *Calgary Daily Herald*, already disgusted with the management of the CPP for its secrecy regarding its operations, condemned the company's production methods. Its editorial decried "Wilful Waste" and warned that the flaring was depleting the oilfield. The paper estimated the daily waste at $1,140 and said the company or the government should find a way to conserve the precious gas.

Archie Dingman, president of CPP, reacted to the *Herald's* charges in its competitor, the *Calgary Morning Albertan*. The *Herald* had waved the "red rag" in spite of the facts, said Dingman, painting CPP as a corporate menace. Department of the Interior employee Stan Slipper investigated and found the plant flaring more than 2 million cubic feet of gas per day. Pressure had dropped to 65 psi from 210 psi, and over 65 percent of the gas in the field was gone. He suggested a pipeline to Calgary or a plant to make carbon black—used in the manufacture of rubber. Ottawa notified CPP of its legal obligation to quit wasting gas but the March 1920 deadline passed and the glow still filled the sky.

Turner Valley's future did not look good. Its major producer could not build a pipeline to Calgary, and the gas company would not connect the new oilfield to its existing system. Others expressed interest in the field. Imperial Oil, a subsidiary of John D. Rockefeller's Standard Oil of New Jersey since 1899, had been searching for oil in the Canadian West for decades. "Everywhere in Canada" was Imperial's slogan, and it wanted in to Alberta's first oilfield. During the Great War, the British government also kept close track of Turner Valley drilling and attempted to keep the Commonwealth resource out of American control by en couraging English investment. Unfortunately, neither the central Canadian markets nor the British investors opened their wallets to keep western Canadian oil under Commonwealth control.

Albertans could not finance the oilfield alone. Herron, Dingman, and a few others struggled to develop properties, but they sometimes failed to make lease rentals and lacked capital to expand their operations. Limping along from one minor finan-cial crisis to another, Turner Valley development was vulnerable to even a minor accident. On October 20, 1920, a CPR steam locomotive compressor blew up at the CPP plant and started a fire. Workers did their best to put out the blaze, but the wooden frame building housing the absorption plant ignited quickly. "The flames soon gained complete control and enveloped the whole building. A supply of gasoline running into a storage tank was closed off, and this prevented any fire from reaching the storage, which would undoubtedly have set fire to the der-ricks. The latter were protected by throwing steam on them." Dingman hurried from Calgary to the site of the uninsured plant and said "That class of building makes it almost impossi-ble to carry insurance on it." The *Calgary Daily Herald* reported "Gasoline Absorption Plant at Dingman Well Destroyed by Fire of Unknown Cause—Loss Reported to Be in Neighborhood of $70,000; Terrific Explosion Occurs When Flames Attack

Gasoline Tanks, Which Shakes Surrounding District." The plant
was a total loss and the company was forced into bankruptcy.

Imperial Oil Buys the Gas Plant

Imperial Oil stepped in. On January 18, 1921, it formed a new
company called Royalite Oil and paid off the old directors of
CPP with a 20 percent share in the new company. Manager John
H. Macleod hired Sam Coultis to design and build a new absorption plant that produced gasoline until 1927. The engineer also
built a compressor station, and the gas company linked a combination six- and eight-inch pipeline from the plant to its main line
at Okotoks. Compressors powered by six, 80-horsepower Clark
gas engines began pumping gas into the line on New Year's Eve
and by January 1, 1922, Calgary was burning Turner Valley gas.
Imperial also built a Calgary refinery in 1922, and doubled the
capacity of its Turner Valley compressor station during 1923.

The development of western Canada's first major oilfield
included many of the elements that became defining character-
istics. The first investors came from central Canada. They hired
Americans to drill the first wells with technology imported from
the United States. Oil and gas quickly took over from wood and
coal as the fuel of choice, thereby changing the infrastructure of
an agriculturally based economy to one controlled by the international dictates of a global petroleum industry. When an independent Canadian oil company failed to attract investors, a
Canadian subsidiary of a massive American petroleum conglom-
erate bought controlling interest in the venture and began operating the oilfield as part of the vertically integrated multinational
corporation's empire.

Explosion at gas plant, Royalties area. (Glenbow Archives, NA-2719-7)

Other Processing Plants in the Early Years

Although the Turner Valley field disappeared from the minds of most people during the war period and until the mid-1920s, a few small companies struggled to exploit petroleum. Several independent oil companies produced oil from a few wells and supplied southern Alberta markets. By 1920 there were more than 20 teamsters including Sam Johnston, Jack Riley, Slim Morehouse, and Frank Coutts making the two-day trip between the oilfield and Okotoks, hauling oil to the train station in large wooden drums with six-horse teams.

Nearby, a few independents operated in the Turner Valley field. Before hiring on with Royalite, Sam G. Coultis designed and built a small still for producing gasoline and kerosene for the Alberta Southern Refining Company. The plant operated successfully for its owners, Pugh and Livingstone, until they sold out to Imperial in 1926. It processed crude oil from the Alberta Southern No. 1 well and the Alberta Southern No. 2 well and sold gasoline for 54 cents a gallon. The Alberta Petroleum Consolidated No. 2 well and the Prudential well provided product for the refinery

Sunset over Turner Valley Gas Plant, 1930s. (Glenbow Archives, NA-67-53).

operated by the Canadian Southern Refining Company. A third plant, run by the Jennings Refining Company Limited, processed product from the Illinois-Alberta well. Finally, Canadian Southern Refining Company built a still and refined natural gas from the Prudential well and Alberta Petroleum Consolidated No. 2 well. Each of these small refineries processed wet gas from shallow wells and stripped off liquids for local sale. Some of the waste gas fired steam boilers at nearby rigs. With no pipelines to Calgary, these small producers only sold their products in barrels to a very small local market. As a result, they never provided much competition to Royalite. Unfortunately, with no markets, most refiners merely flared the waste gas, turning night into day in the oilfield.

Sour Gas and the Turner Valley Gas Plant

There were legitimate reasons for flaring, at least in the early years. Royalite No. 4 produced a sour gas that could not be sold to consumers without processing. Until Royalite built its scrubbing plant in 1925, the deadly gas from the new well was useless. The Union Gas Company of Toronto built Canada's first scrubbing plant for natural gas in 1924 to remove hydrogen sulphide from Ontario gas. It used the Seaboard Process originally developed by the Koppers Company of Pittsburgh to make coal gas safe for customers. Royalite plant manager Sam Coultis adapted the Seaboard Process for the Turner Valley plant. He designed a tall steel tower filled with a honeycomb of redwood slats. Sour gas entered the bottom of the tower and percolated up while a watery solution of soda ash trickled down from the top, clinging to the wood. By the time the gas reached the top, it was "sweet," or clean. The deadly hydrogen sulphide left the tower in the soda ash solution. In a reactivating tower it trickled down again while air sucked off the deadly gas. Expansions to this system allowed it to process 60 million cubic feet of gas per day in 1928, 75 million cubic feet of gas per day in 1935, and 100 million cubic feet of gas per day in 1941 for wartime demand. In 1935, the wooden trays in the sour gas scrubbers were replaced with steel plates. Decades later, Sam Coultis was still hesitant to admit what they did with the hydrogen sulphide: "Those tall smoke stacks that used to be there, they got a lot of it." Indeed, from 1925 until Royalite installed a sulphur plant in 1952, powerful fans merely mixed the deadly hydrogen sulphide gas with air and disposed of the problem in the manner typical of the times: dilution was the solution. In 1925, Royalite also imported another used absorption plant from C.F. Brown and Company of Alhambra, California.

Gas Storage in an Old Gas Field

Once Royalite figured out how to clean the sour gas, it had to deal with excess production during warm months. During 1930, ostensibly as a conservation measure but also as an attractive income generator, the company began pumping surplus scrubbed gas down the pipeline to the Bow Island field. Although consumers demanded large amounts of gas in the winter, companies routinely flared gas during the summer. Storing it in the Bow Island reservoir gave a secure source of extra gas for the winter months and a new source of income to the gas company and Royalite.

Exploration and development in Turner Valley virtually shut down during the early 1930s, but the plant kept processing gas and sending it to market. As gas pressure dropped in the Turner Valley field in the late 1920s and early 1930s, the Smith Separators and small compressor plants became less and less capable of stripping the gasoline from the wet gas. Royalite shut down its old absorption plant in 1927. In 1933, it hired Charlie "High Pressure" Ward, a native of Oklahoma, to build a new system. Ward's nickname came from the time he exploded a separator with too much gas pressure. At the Turner Valley field, he installed a system capable of handling the relatively high-pressure gas efficiently. Wet gas rose from the bottom of the absorption towers, percolating up through bubble caps on plates covered in lean oil.

The gas plant's absorber, lean oil pumphouse, and gasoline buildings and other facilities were the major elements of the 1933 high-pressure lean oil absorption plant. They represent an important part of the history of Turner Valley as they were part of the first such plant in Canada. Three other smaller plants once operated in the field, but only the Turner Valley plant is still there. Operational for 52 years, it was the longest running absorption plant in Canada and one of the oldest operational plants of its kind in North America.

Others watched with interest as Royalite began operating the first Canadian high-pressure lean oil absorption unit. In 1934, rancher A.H. Mayland, owner of Gas and Oil Products Limited, erected a used absorber plant from the United States on a site just southeast of Hartell. The California-built equipment provided the first competition for the Royalite-dominated field in early August 1934, but its daily capacity of processing 80,000 cubic feet of gas was little more than token competition. The British American Oil Ltd. also imported a used plant—theirs was from Coutts, Montana—and placed it on a site near Longview in 1936. The $400,000 plant provided another alternative to the Royalite monopoly on gas and oil refining in the oilfield. Royalite reacted to the rapid development in the south end of the valley in 1935 by building an absorption plant with machinery taken from the Turner Valley plant. Ten used absorbers gave the new plant a capacity of 60,000 cubic feet per day. The main plant received four "new large high-pressure absorbers of Canadian manufacture."

The *Western Oil Examiner*, a Calgary-based newspaper, always jumped on a story. It spoke out often against Royalite's monopolistic control of Turner Valley production. In 1934, it noted that Imperial had once again arbitrarily cut the price it paid to naphtha producers. The Oil and Gas Shareholders Association investigated the unilateral action and its negative effects on its members. Calls for an investigation against Imperial and its subsidiary continued through the 1930s, eventually culminating in the Alberta government creating a Royal Commission to review the petroleum industry in 1938. Although the commission's report in 1940 found no evidence of unfair prices or practices in the field, the inquiry gave a detailed account of the state of Turner Valley oilfield operations at the time. Conservation measures drastically limited the amount of gas producers could flare, effectively preventing companies with no markets for their gas—anyone other than Royalite—from processing wet gas. As a result, the Alberta government forced Imperial to create a public utility to operate its pipeline and to share it with other producers.

Access to Markets

What to do with the oil and gas once discovered, processed, and ready for market was a problem from the earliest days of the Turner Valley development process. For decades oilfield boosters lobbied governments and companies for a link to the outside world. A few visionaries predicted the growing importance of oil in international relations. In late 1929, under the prophetic headline "Possession of Petroleum Deciding Factor in War," the *Western Oil Examiner* out of Calgary suggested:

> Petroleum will largely govern the fortunes of nations in the years to come. Already it is the cause of one of the greatest fights for possession that the world has ever witnessed. Armies, navies, money, even population, will count as nothing against it. We are all for peace; we want no more of that horror that ended now eleven years ago. But, if war should ever again be visited upon an unhappy world, it will be decided by petroleum. The present effort to control supplies is more gripping than any drama ever written.

The same publication reviewed other Alberta fuel sources before speculating on the province's petroleum future:

> But besides coal we have been tapping an immense potential wealth in oil and gas. We led the production of petroleum, which is a relatively recent development and no man knows when we will strike a crude oil gusher field which will startle the world. We have every evidence that a tremendous oil field, which would one day supply the whole of Canada will result from the discovery operations now in hand.

Turner Valley became that "crude oil gusher field" in 1936, and upon its promise, Imperial Oil continued the search for petroleum that eventually discovered Leduc in 1947 and many more massive oilfields in the late 1940s and 1950s. In the meantime, the Second World War proved the value of Turner Valley's resources.

Plant Expansion During the Second World War

The Second World War caused Turner Valley's largest boom. Maximum production became the order of the day. The Turner Valley gas plant added a Girbotol natural gas sweetener in 1941 to augment the older Seaboard-Koppers scrubber. In 1942, it installed butane splitters to extract isobutane to help make aviation fuel. That same year Alberta production peaked at over 10 million barrels per year, most of it from Turner Valley. And in 1945, Royalite established another subsidiary, Madison Natural Gas Company, to handle Turner Valley gas.

In addition to expanded facilities at the gas plant, the war placed incredible pressure on the Turner Valley oilfield. At the

Turner Valley Gas Plant, 1920s. (Glenbow Archives, NA-711-39)

end of 1939, with Turner Valley producing at full volume, the *Oil Bulletin* reviewed the oilfield's success. With nearly 100 wells producing oil—all but four drilled in the oil-bearing area produced crude—field production had doubled every year since 1936 and experts were predicting "an ultimate recovery of about 200 million barrels with an average recovery per acre of about 15,000 barrels."

The article predicted good things for the future. Turner Valley was almost certainly but one of a series of similar oilfields along the foothills, and wildcat wells in other parts of Alberta had found three new promising, if not spectacular, fields.

> At the end of 1939 drilling or survey-preparatory-to-drilling were underway at some twenty field, many of which already show some commercial oil production or good prospects of production. 1940, in the opinion of many observers, will very probably witness the proving of at least one field to rival the great Turner Valley. To the Wildcatters who make the strike will probably go riches beside which the cost of development will appear infinitesimal. To the oil industry the major strike will probably mean the end of the Marketing Problem. The dream of pipelines over the Rockies and to the Great Lakes will become a reality and Alberta's oil will flow to every part of the Dominion and perhaps beyond.

Unfortunately, the next big Alberta find did not come until early 1947, long after the end of the Second World War. In the meantime, Canada needed as much oil as industry could produce. Under wartime emergency powers, Ottawa appointed George Cottrelle as Dominion Oil Controller on June 29, 1940.

The *Oil Bulletin* later sang praises for the new position in an article titled: "Oil Controller Cottrelle Given Almost Dictatorial Power Over Oil Industry, Oilmen Pleased!" An order-in-council gave Cottrelle power to seize oil anywhere in Canada, the right to find, produce and transport it, the power to advance government money to companies to encourage them to drill for oil, the right to request information from all parts of the industry, the power to over-ride contracts, and the right to construct and add to refineries and gas plants. "Persons or companies failing to observe orders of the Oil Controller may be found guilty of an offence and punished. Alberta oilmen, in general, however, feel that any steps that may be taken by the controller will be for the best interests of the country-at-war, and that such steps will work towards the advancement and betterment of the oil industry."

As war continued, the giddiness of the boom subsided. The oil controller eventually rationed gasoline. Instead of gaining on the enemies of civilization, things seemed to deteriorate as 1942 approached. On December 27, 1941, the *Oil Bulletin* warned: "Allied Oil Tankers attacked, at least one sunk, within sight of the Pacific Coast. An enemy submarine sighted and sunk by American Air Patrols off the Washington Coast. Tankers diverted from the Atlantic to supply expanding American Naval needs in the Pacific. Headlines all from the news of the past few days, they drive home the nearness of the conflict in which we and our Allies are fighting for our very existence."

As the situation grew more desperate, Ottawa raised the rewards for companies willing to drill in Turner Valley. In March 1942, it allowed Ace Royalties No. 2, drilling at the north end of the field, a $25,000 tax concession to encourage it to find more Turner Valley oil. That same month a call came from the Americans. "The United States Government has called Turner

Valley into action against the Japs." The Alaska Highway Route, an inland link to Alaska from Dawson Creek, decided on only two weeks before, promised a safer highway than one vulnerable to Japanese invasion along the Pacific Coast. Imperial Oil Ltd. and British American Oil Company pressed their refineries to the limit in Calgary, making gasoline and aviation fuel from Turner Valley crude. Motor oil and grease for the operation came from other sources. The companies shipped these products to the end of the track at Dawson Creek in tank cars where a hundred trucks worked around the clock moving gas and oil 390 miles further northwest to Fort Nelson in steel drums. Thousands of barrels of product went into building the road, and trucks using the route burned much more. "The Alaska Road provides another example of the increasing military importance of Turner Valley and other proven and potential oilfields in Alberta."

The aviation gasoline mentioned went in part to help build the highway, fuelling planes that went ahead, making a route and establishing a line of airstrips. But most of the aviation gas went to planes in the British Commonwealth Air Training Plan, a program that consumed 2 million gallons of 87-octane gas each year, most of it from Turner Valley. By the end of the year western Canadian refineries were ready to produce the "fighting grade 100-octane from the high grade of Turner Valley." Royalite's subsidiary, Valley Pipeline Company Ltd., contracted Horton Steel Works Limited of Fort Erie, Ontario, to construct two spherical containers on the west side of the plant to help with this program. Built in 1942, they stored isobutane, a by-product of gas processing and a valuable ingredient in aviation gasoline. Horton built the first Hortonspheres at Port Arthur, Texas, in 1923, riveting together a high-pressure vessel. Welded joints replaced rivets in 1932. The Hortonspheres at Turner Valley were 38 feet in diameter,

supported by eight, 28-foot-high legs on concrete footings. The
⅝-inch-thick steel allowed the spheres to operate at an internal
pressure of 48 pounds per square inch and hold 5,000 barrels
of product. The first in western Canada, the Hortonspheres cost
about $50,000 to build in the fall of 1942.

The last issue of the *Oil Bulletin* in 1942 warned that although Turner Valley was producing at maximum capacity, it
could and should do more. Only two thirds of available rigs were
on the job and there were still 90 drilling sites in "proven territory"
that would almost certainly add to oil production. Various factors
kept the rigs from contributing to the war effort. Companies were
not drilling because the price of oil was artificially low due to wartime price controls, tax burdens, and royalty payments. Unless the
government changed these factors, or financed wells itself, Carl
Nickle could not see much chance for more production from
western oilfields in general, particularly from Turner Valley.

In early 1943, Ottawa implemented a series of changes. It
eliminated import duties, war tax and sales tax on oil equipment,
and created a 40 percent write-off provision on exploration wells
and dry holes. The oil controller also raised the price of Turner
Valley oil by 15 cents per barrel. Finally, on April 9, 1943, in
an unprecedented step, Ottawa established Wartime Oils. This
unique federal program financed exploration drilling around the
Turner Valley under extremely favourable conditions: Ottawa paid
all drilling costs and companies only had to repay the loan if they
found oil. The program lasted two years. By the end of 1943, this
series of changes contributed to a record 115 well completions.

Working Conditions During the War

The Second World War caused Turner Valley's largest boom, but

Gas flares from Home Oil well. (Glenbow Archives, NA-4062-6)

wartime conditions made it less freewheeling than the previous booms. Overnight, things tightened. A chain link fence topped with barbed wire sprang up around the gas plant. Armed guards patrolled the perimeter day and night. Everyone was on edge. Geoff Andrews remembered people talking about "when the Japs come over the hills," but there was relatively little chance of invasion. Sabotage was the greatest fear. A searchlight on top of the water tower, at the present location of the 14th fairway, played on the plant at night. Floodlights replaced the searchlight after the war.

The day Canada entered the Second World War a guard challenged Ralph Steen when he returned to the plant at the end of the day. For the remainder of the war employees had to sign in and out each time they entered or left the plants. The plant appointed an ex-RCMP officer, Mr. Gow, as chief of plant security. Once, an operator in the field asked Mr. Trammel, the Royalite manager, for his security card. Trammel produced his and then asked the operator to do the same. When he could not show his own card, Trammel suspended him for a week. Howard Harris was a guard at the plant during the war and once accidentally sat on the alarm button in one of the guard shacks and put his fellow guards into a fright. They carried photo identification badges and memorized a password to get into the plant. The guards also carried shotguns, as did each operator in the plant and the men walking the pipelines. Tom Trotter recalled that each supervisor carried a Model 94 .3030 Winchester rifle. Other oilfield operations went unguarded. There were no security guards on the rigs during the war.

Geoff Andrews did not need a security pass because he worked at the machine shop north of the plant. The shop was very busy, running two shifts and building many things that were not available due to the war's demand on the industrial capacity of the country. They reworked old cable tool steel into new tools at the blacksmith's shop. Old bits, up to 24 inches in diameter, melted in the forge and became the raw metal for new tools.

Coverage for some shortages could be improved, some could not. During the war the Royalite office hired women, unheard of before 1939 when men filled even the secretarial jobs. Women drove buses for the oil companies, delivering crews to drilling rigs and other locations on shift changes. The buses were often improvised; Gerry Schultz built boxes for the back of trucks to convert them into buses during the war. Seats came from streetcars the city of Calgary no longer used. Rationed tires were a major problem, keeping many vehicles off the road. "Red" Kennedy—a nickname earned for his flaming red hair—had to get out into the field often, but even his position at the plant did not make the effort any easier. The plant trucks and cars often ran on old, bald, and fraying tires. Red once had four flat tires in one day and had to abandon his vehicle and walk back to the plant warehouse.

As serious as the war was, it also had a lighter side. Melvina Briggs recalled that women feared invasion in the early months. "We young wives used to worry. We thought that perhaps we might be bombed because it was a vital industry." Those men not at war trained for a home guard. In case of invasion, these men would serve as the last line of defence. However, during training in the foothills west of Turner Valley, the home guard got lost and could not find their way home. The women never let them live down the humiliation.

With time, plant security became a bit of a joke, to some. One Royalite employee faithfully showed his security pass, complete with a picture of Hitler neatly pasted over his own mug shot. The same fellow made a game of taunting the searchlight operator, running through the edge of the beam of light, then dashing off behind a tank or building, teasing the man with hints of unauthorised movement. One woman made a game of visiting the men at the fenced plant grounds, pushing peanuts through the chain links, talking to the guards as if they were monkeys in the zoo.

Although most eligible men enlisted, Turner Valley oil was important to the war effort too. One day Gerry Schultz showed up at the cafe where his sweetheart Mildred Gimbel worked in the south end of the oilfield and whisked her off to get married. The war effort had called his boss, Gene Denton of Drilling Contractors, trying to force Gerry to go overseas. Gene called him in on July 5, 1940, and asked "Hand, were you planning to get married?" He was, so Gerry borrowed a shirt and headed off to find Mildred. Gene said "And hurry back because there's a war on." Off to Calgary they went, picking up Gerry's mother and sister on the way to the wedding. Then it was back to work on the rigs for Gerry, slinging hash and pouring coffee for Mildred.

Working Conditions

In the oilfield, the heightened level of demand for oil created the biggest boom ever. Even more than before, the town of Turner Valley was the centre of the oilfield and the gas plant the centre of operations for the drilling and collection of petroleum products. The plant processed a variety of light petroleum products, and pipelines transported oil to the Calgary refineries. Gladys Lake lived nearby and recalled the significance of the plant to the community. "We lived down there, beside the plant, where the noise was all the time. If the plant went down, which it very seldom did, except for cleaning, you missed it."

Although the gas plant was a busy place, its operations were simple: it served as a collecting site for oil and gas from the entire oilfield. The compressor plant increased gas pressure before forcing the sour gas through scrubbing systems which removed deadly hydrogen sulphide so the gas could go through pipelines to the gas company's southern Alberta customers. The butane splitters installed to extract isobutane to help make aviation fuel in 1942 were the only new part of the plant added during the war other than the Horton Spheres.

As busy and industrial as the site appeared to people looking through the chain link fence, it was a fairly simple place to work. Operators were in charge of a building, making sure the equipment in their care functioned properly. They sometimes had an assistant. But most of the work around the plant involved routine maintenance, changing charts, oiling machinery, checking pressure gauges, and not falling asleep.

In the early years, most aspects of work and production were unregulated. In general, Turner Valley employees treated their workers paternalistically—they took care of the workers fairly well and expected governments to leave them alone. Oil companies hired drilling contractors and they, in turn, hired staff for the rigs. In the early days, skilled labour was scarce and the mostly American crews worked as teams, drilling wells according to their own preferred methods. Shift work was common, but 12-hour shifts, seven days a week took their toll. The long shifts also prevented other workers from learning new jobs, a sore point at many times during the development process. Still, all went fairly well during booms. But when the inevitable busts came, the unemployed complained about the lack of work and called for regulations.

Those looking for work saw an obvious solution to their problem: enforce the nine-hour day and create new jobs. So they appealed to the provincial government. The Alberta Factory Act controlled hours of work in the oilfield and the 1926 law limited drilling crews to nine-hour work days. But 12-hour shifts continued. Judge A.A. Carpenter investigated the situation in December 1926, and American drillers W.V. Nicholson and Clarence Snyder pointed out that most California drillers worked an eight-hour day. Drillers lobbied for the shorter shifts in 1927. Experience elsewhere proved that the eight-hour shifts did not create extra expense for the companies. Shorter shifts increased performance and contributed to workplace safety. In spite of the evidence, Turner Valley companies continued 12-hour shifts. Due to an oversight in the Factory Act, oil and gas wells were exempt from the law.

Gas plant employees worked 10-hour days until 1928 when their co-workers from the Imperial Oil Co. refinery came out from Calgary to install new equipment. Jack Seeman was a general labourer at the plant at the time and he rubbed shoulders with the Calgary men. "The steel workers belonged to a union and worked eight hours a day, so that wasn't a very good combination with us labour men working a 10-hour day. It wasn't long before we went on an eight-hour day and our wages were raised to five dollars a day for labour work." After the eight-hour day became common, workers agitated for a six-day week. One Lord's Day Act case went to court, but it was overturned and the seven-day work week continued. Efforts to create a more reasonable work week for oilfield labour ended in the early 1930s when many lost their jobs.

When the next boom erupted in 1936, the unemployed once again asked for a chance to make a living. They asked the government to enforce the forty-hour week and a provincial board of inquiry chaired by Clayton Adams recommended the shorter work-week. But the Alberta Producers' Association rejected the shorter work-week. It boiled down to a struggle for power between the unemployed, the companies, and the workers. According to a government report in May, 1937, 654 unemployed workers signed a petition asking for the forty-hour week to create more jobs. Supported by the companies, 350 employed workers signed a counter-petition of their own. Finally, on June 30, 1937, the provincial board of industrial relations made a special ruling for the Turner Valley oilfield: drillers would work a 56-hour week and all other oilpatch workers would work a 48-hour week. This special decision exempted the oilfield from Section 10 of the Alberta Hours of Work Act.

But the issue did not go away. In 1938, W.D. King, Deputy

Minister of the Department of Trade and Industry for Alberta, suggested the eight-hour day as a way of creating oilfield employment. The province supported the shorter day again in 1939; companies and workers opposed it and the unemployed supported the job-creating program. War changed everything. When men left for battle, the unemployment problem vanished, labour became scarce and the Board of Industrial Relations relaxed peacetime regulations. Oilfield employees worked long hours, long weeks, and often went without days off for months at a time. Companies paid regular wages for overtime during the war.

The hours of work debate in Turner Valley apparently had more to do with a power struggle between oilfield operators and the governments than with economics, safety or employment. Imperial Oil never liked government interference in its operations. It saw itself as a benevolent employer, an omniscient producer, and an international force powerful enough to effect change in provincial and national politics. As a result, it frequently ignored or challenged legislation or blamed government intervention in its operations for production problems. During the inquiry into Imperial Oil's control over the Turner Valley oilfield—the McGillivray Royal Commission into Alberta's Oil Industry—a *Turner Valley Flare* editorial stated that Royalite and Imperial were refusing to drill new wells because they felt pressured by the commission. The editorial blamed the lack of expansion and the resulting unemployment on the intrusion by government regulation into the oil industry.

The Royal Commission recommended the government create a public utility to manage pipelines in Alberta, taking away the monopolistic position held by Imperial Oil. This the government did. But Imperial won much more than it lost. The inquiry called many witnesses and investigated and discussed all aspects of exploration, production, pricing, transportation, refining, marketing, taxation, and conservation. Ultimately, McGillivray's findings supported Imperial's objection to government interference:

> We repeat for the sake of clarity and emphasis, that which we have before said that no case has been made out for government intervention in Alberta, in any branch of the petroleum industry, including marketing, as to which we are specifically directed to report. In such circumstances there is not the slightest occasion for the government to exercise control for the protection of the public. On the contrary it would seem that the public in Alberta is adequately protected by the play of contending forces prompted by desire for gain.

Imperial's opposition to government control over its operations was entirely consistent with its role as part of a vertically integrated multinational oil company, Standard Oil of New Jersey. Alberta's newly created Conservation Board was threatening Imperial's activities in Turner Valley, and the corporation saw the McGillivray Commission's conclusions as a way to prevent further provincial government incursion into the industry.

Training and Education

Although gas plant employees worked with dangerous materials under high-pressure, most of them had little formal training. Only steam engineers needed a provincial certificate, and it merely proved their ability to handle a steam boiler. Other workers learned the job on the job. Jim Donnelly, for example, started with Royalite as a roustabout in 1951. He worked his way into the scrubbing plant, compressor plant, propane

Stock brokerage salesman at Major No. 4 well, 1942. (Provincial Archives of Alberta, P1286)

plant and gas plant, learning the skills of an operator as he went. He recalled that most men trained under an operator for a few months before taking over his jobs. Others had just a few days' overlap. Jim eventually took a fourth-class steam course by correspondence from the Southern Alberta Institute of Technology in Calgary.

Bill McGonigle also worked his way up through the jobs at the plant. Part of the routine involved driving the field, changing charts in the meters, and doing routine maintenance. He said the trucks carried chains and shovels in case they got stuck. Some trucks even had emergency food supplies but he never had to rely on the emergency rations. He once had to walk over half a mile in bitterly cold weather to check a battery, a collection point in the gathering system. The roads were not built up and they got drifted in quite often. One time the snow came into the road almost as fast as he could shovel a track for his truck. He worked as an operator in each part of the plant until he retired in 1976.

After the War: New Life for an Old Plant

Just as the Royalite plant began showing signs of aging, management decided to pour money into upgrading the facility and adding new processes to the site. It opened a sulphur plant on site in 1952 and moved in a used propane plant the same year. These two operations allowed the plant to make new products for sale to new markets, and they assured the plant's financial viability for many more years.

Rotten egg smell was an unfortunate by-product of the oil and gas industry in Turner Valley from the earliest days. Even the Dingman discovery well's sweet gas included traces of sulphur. Anyone burning Turner Valley gasoline in their automobile advertised the Alberta oilfield's products wherever they drove. Oilpatch residents quickly became accustomed to the smell they associated with their careers, but others did not like the stench. One woman's sisters would not let her hang her clothes in their closets when she visited Calgary because her clothing stank of sulphur. Prevailing westerly winds usually diluted the smell and carried it far to the east where it gradually disappeared before it hit the Saskatchewan border. But the smell got much worse in 1924. Royalite No. 4's discovery was great news for the company and for natural gas customers in southern Alberta, but the scrubbing plant merely mixed the hydrogen sulphide with air and dumped it out the top of tall towers. No one knows the full consequences of this pollution, but for more than two decades people downwind of the plant inhaled diluted hydrogen sulphide and lived with its deposits on everything they touched and ate.

Finally, in 1952, economic conditions changed and Royalite suddenly realized an untapped potential for the vented hydrogen sulphide and solved a local public relations problem at the same time. "Operation Brimstone" began running the acid gas through a sulphur plant at midnight, Friday, July 11, 1952. Production averaged 27 tons per day by 1955, topping 40 tons per day when natural gas users demanded high gas volumes during cold winter periods. Sulphur-laden gas from the scrubbing plant first went through a 1,600°F reactor furnace where some of the sulphur came off as a liquid. The sour gases that resulted from this process then went through a 550 to 650°F converter and a catalyst— pelleted activated bauxite—and most of the rest of the sulphur came out of the gas. Molten sulphur from both stages then went into a pit, 40 x 50 feet, where the red liquid cooled to its classic brilliant yellow solid state. When market demands dictated, workers drilled holes in the block, inserted dynamite, and broke it up into smaller chunks. A bulldozer loaded it into a crusher and workers bagged it or loaded it in powdered form onto trucks headed for railway cars at Okotoks. Some sulphur in stick form went to the Far East, but most Turner Valley sulphur in the early days went to mining operations, sugar refining, insecticides, pulp and paper manufacturing, rubber making, explosives, and many other applications.

The *Royalite Oil Reporter* concluded an article about the sulphur plant with an explanation of the significance of the plant to community social life: "And as far as the good ladies are concerned, 'Operation Brimstone' has reduced 'Operation Silver Polish' just in time to avert a civil war."

Propane was not as offensive to the nose as sulphur, but Royalite also added its recovery to the operations at the Turner Valley gas plant in 1952. Royalite purchased Western Propane

Limited's nearby plant in the summer and moved the facility—in operation since 1948—to the plant site in the fall. On October 20, 1952, Royalite's Propane Division began stripping propane from the gas as it flowed into the plant. After a chemical process that the company's chief chemical engineer A.G.A. Piercey summarized in a mere five pages of text, diagrams and formulas for the *Royalite Oil Reporter* in December 1952, liquid propane went into storage tanks before trucks delivered it to customers or the company's propane terminal in Calgary. Production that month averaged 18,000 Imperial gallons each day.

Production Methods Lengthened Life of Field

Gas flows and oil production peaked in the Turner Valley field during the Second World War, but demand for petroleum products rose quickly as society became addicted to the internal combustion engine. As a result, companies began considering methods to boost production. Injecting water into the bottom of the reservoir and increasing pressure on the oil to move to the wellhead was a simple form of enhanced recovery. A Royalite pilot project met success in Turner Valley in 1948 and further injection and flooding projects helped with production in 1958 and 1960.

Increasing pressure in the field meant all wells would benefit. Although the Alberta government suggested unitization for the Turner Valley field as early as the 1930s, companies refused. Unitization would have prevented the waste of the gas and extended the life of the oilfield by operating all the wells as a group—a unit—thereby preserving gas pressure which served as a motive force to move liquid oil to the wells. Most operators chose, instead, to produce their wells as quickly as possible, flaring waste gas and reaping immediate economic rewards. These short-sighted methods wasted most of the gas in the field and drastically reduced its potential. In 1950, the government passed the Turner Valley Unit Operations Act, and in 1957, new provisions in the Oil and Gas Conservation Act gave the Conservation Board the power to regulate unitized groups of wells, assuring each well owner a fair share of the proceeds from the unit. Units finally began operating in 1958, and by 1962, the whole field was divided into seven units. After decades of wilful obstinacy, the various companies agreed to co-operate to save what was left of the oil and gas in the field. A single company managed each unit for the owners, injecting water into some wells along the western or downdip end of the field and producing oil and gas in an efficient manner from the rest of the wells.

Stable Gas Plant Production

Canada's first big gas plant aged slowly. While flashy new facilities sprang up at Leduc, Redwater, Pembina, and elsewhere in the Canadian West, the Turner Valley plant outlived its expected life. It even outlasted its creators and many of the men that worked in it during its busiest period in the Second World War. It outlived Royalite and became part of many larger corporate empires before it processed its last gas in 1985. Calgary Petroleum Products sold out to Imperial in 1920, and its subsidiary Royalite sold the plant to Dominion Securities in 1948. In 1949, the plant became part of the Bronfman family business empire, and British American—Gulf Canada—bought the facility in 1962. The plant passed into the hands of its last owner, Western Decalta (1977) Ltd., in 1977.

Old age affected the plant in many ways. Some parts of the machinery date to the 1930s and many of the underground pipelines and storage tanks appear on no maps of the site. For decades, the location of many features was kept in the minds of the engineers and maintenance personnel. Unfortunately, most of them have passed away. Elmer Andersen recalled that in later years workers cannibalized machinery in other parts of the oilfield to keep the gas plant alive. Jim Donnelly remembered workers taking parts from one compressor in the plant to repair another unit. According to Ruth Pearson, general housekeeping and cleaning of the plant office began in the early 1970s and many plant records were burned. Only the most obvious operational materials survived this purge. When the plant closed in 1985, some records made their way into archives but much valuable information went to the local dump. Only the quick wits and hard work of local history buffs in Turner Valley saved the day: historically minded men and women literally climbed into a pit and salvaged records.

A Good Secure Job

Jim McInnis took a job on Friday, August 13, 1943, to help Royalite build an extension on the gas plant. When a Royalite man showed up in Winnipeg recruiting for the plant, he jumped at the chance. Previously a grain buyer, he moved to Turner Valley to escape the grain dust that bothered his lungs. The other men just shook their heads when he arrived in Turner Valley, telling him he was foolish to begin a new career in a plant obviously past its prime. But Jim trained on the job, eventually became an operator, and ended his career at the plant. Some feared the oil industry, seeing it as an insecure employer, but for many men the Turner Valley gas plant was not only the centre of Alberta's first oilfield, it was a reliable source of income for many years and allowed them to retire with secure pensions.

Chapter 3

Pipelining Projects

With no railway tracks to move oil and gas products to market, Royalite quickly pushed for the first of many pipelines. Its monopoly on sales of natural gas to Canadian Western Natural Gas created a long-term market that justified the expense of a permanent link to the gas company's mainline in Okotoks. So in 1921, Turner Valley gas began surging through a line six and eight inches in diameter. In spite of its capacity, it eventually ran out of room. The gas company then built a new 10-inch gas pipeline directly to Calgary in 1925. In 1926, Alberta natural gas production surpassed Ontario's for the first time and the western Canadian oilpatch never looked back. The gas company added another gas pipeline to Calgary in 1928, this one 14 inches in diameter. For a time, Royalite used five large tank trucks with a daily capacity of 27,000 gallons to move oil from the oilfield to railhead at Okotoks. Finally, in 1925, it built a four-inch welded pipeline to move oil directly from the Royalite No. 4 well to the refinery Imperial Oil had opened in 1922 on the banks of the Bow River in southwest Calgary. Railways started converting from coal to petroleum fuels this decade after oil-electric locomotives began pulling trains in 1926. The *Western Oil Examiner* noticed the trend and predicted new markets for the Alberta petroleum industry.

Canada's First Major Pipeline

Today, pipeline construction has become big business, with large diameter lines moving oil and gas across continents. But in the early days pipelines were small, short, and often messy. Canadian Western's first long-distance pipeline was built in only 86 days during the spring and summer of 1912. The 16-inch line, 172 miles long, transported gas from Bow Island to Calgary and served other communities along the way. The gas arrived in Calgary on July 17, 1912, under its own pressure, and 12,000 Calgarians attended the opening ceremonies which included the lighting of a flare.

Pipeline engineers shudder when their publicity colleagues plan grandiose public events to celebrate construction projects because unforeseen problems often delay official launches. Such was the case with the first gas pipeline to Calgary. As supervisor for the pipeline at the time, P.D. Mellon recalled an explosion in the pipeline that almost squelched the celebration. "Early that afternoon the line blew up in a slough near DeWinton. Things looked pretty gloomy but we rushed several gangs of men down there and we were able to get the line coupled up again and the pressure built up."

That evening the celebration went ahead as planned. "Eugene Coste and his wife were there and Whitey Foster was in charge of

South Turner Valley oilfield, June 28, 1937. (Provincial Archives of Alberta, P1800)

the valve control. At a signal from Mr. Coste, Whitey turned on the valve and he turned it on plenty, because coming out of this standpipe there was a tremendous amount of dust, then stones and great big boulders, two or three pairs of overalls, pieces of skids, almost everything came out." Mrs. Coste set the gas flare on fire with a Roman candle. "Then Mr. Coste signalled to turn it down. Whitey thought he meant to turn her on more. Whitey opened her up again and this almost caused a panic. People were backing up into each other and yelling at this terrible flare going up into the air."

On July 24, 1912, gas began flowing to customers. The *Calgary Daily Herald* stated: "This morning marked a new epoch in the history of lighting and heating insofar as gas is concerned in Calgary. Artificial gas in the city is now a thing of the past. The ringing out of the old and ringing in of the new has taken place, and the natural product has supplanted the artificial."

Harsh Realities of Pipeline Construction

Behind the scenes, laying pipeline was less glamorous. Pipes must be buried to protect them from the elements. In particular, they have to be below frost level, which can sink quite deep in cold winters. By the end of the 1920s, Royalite had a mechanical ditcher—a trenching machine—to help install the pipelines. But for many years before and after these machines began clawing out neat trenches, men dug them by hand. Pipelines did not always go the most convenient route either, often just the most direct, and that meant digging through hard packed soil, gravel, or rock. Geoff Andrews remembered working on the bull gang, doing whatever job the foreman dictated. He spent his first summer on the "banjo and anchor" or the round-nosed shovel and pick, digging trenches.

Digging holes or trenches by hand is tough work. The green-horn often works too fast, wearing out quickly. The trick to most hard manual labour is to develop a pace you can sustain for the entire day—without tiring. Steady lifting of the pick far over-head and dropping it with accuracy is far more successful than wild swinging with powerful blows. Once the pick breaks up the ground, the foot pushes the shovel into the soil. A bend in the knees gets the legs involved in the lifting, using the whole body to throw the dirt and rocks and gravel out of the trench into the pile beside the pipeline. Hour after hour after day after week, the rhythm continued, digging a trench to a new refinery or distant well. Over rocky hills, through soggy swamps, and across gravel-filled valleys, the men removed thousands of cubic feet of dirt from the ground.

Once the trench was dug, four or five feet deep, the men set aside their picks and shovels for the heavy work. Wooden-wheeled wagons loaded with sections of pipe came from the nearest railway siding at Okotoks. Pulled by teams of horses and later by steam or diesel tractors on steel wheels, thousands of sections of pipe moved slowly across the countryside. Men walked alongside, removing lengths by hand, dropping them in place by the open trench. Each section often weighed as much or more than a man, so moving the steel required skill to avoid injury. Since contract or day labour did much of the heavy construction, an injured back meant loss of income or even the end to a career.

After distributing pipe along the trench, the men began bending and joining it before preparing to lower it into the ground. The early pipe was small, only three or four inches in diameter. Threaded ends spun together by hand. Once relatively secured, chain tools clamped onto the pipe and tightened the threads until they were leakproof. At first the pipes were lowered into the trenches unprotected, but the steel rusted quickly. Various systems helped protect the pipe from the elements. Lawrence Barker hired on with Royalite in April 1929 with a promise of a month's work. He stayed 40 years and five months. When he worked on pipeline crews, they covered the pipe with grease or tar, lowered it into the ground and then backfilled the trench by hand.

Red Kennedy started his 37-year career with Royalite on the bull gang too. It was not a secure job. At one point, the foreman fired lazy men each afternoon and replaced them with more energetic ones the next morning. Red laid pipe from one- to six-inches size, all screwed together by hand. Before lowering it into the trench, they tarred the pipe, wrapped it with gunny sack material, then tarred it again. After lowering the sticky line into the ground, they grabbed their shovels and threw the rocks and dirt back into the hole.

George de Mille and hundreds more like him worked the

pipeline crews. Picks and shovels became old friends, but the "wiper's" job was the least popular. One man stood on each side of the wrapped pipe, holding ends of a width of gunny-sack material called the "granny-rag." The "wiper" walked alongside the pipe with the bucket of gooey tar, and as the men flapped the cloth back and forth, the "wiper" applied more black goop to the pipe. Invariably, the "wiper" ended up dirtier than the pipe, and his clothing got so encrusted with tar, dirt, and grime that his coveralls stood up by themselves.

Ernie Carter claimed the hardest work he ever did was installing pipelines. He helped coat them with tar and burlap too. "I guess it stood up pretty well, if it was properly treated. But a lot of people would go to great trouble to coat the pipe and then drop it in the hole and come back and drop rocks on it and break the darned stuff through to the metal again. Of course then it started to rust." For a time, nothing showed. Then one day the pipe broke. "You would have maybe a few hundred barrels an hour running down a ditch for several hours before you discovered it. So it made a mess." The crews cleaned up as best they could, then burned the oil in a pit. "That was the solution in those days for a lot of things; if you didn't know what to do with it, you burnt it."

The bull gang often filled the trenches by hand, but with time the operation became more mechanized. The trenchers cut the gap for the pipe, welders mated the pipe with solid joints, wrapping machines coated and sealed the pipe against moisture to reduce rusting, and tractors pulled equipment that placed the pipe in the trench, backfilled the trench, and flattened the right-of-way. Although mechanization sped up the operation, it did not always ensure stable employment. For example, Albert Smith's work on the 1925 gas pipeline project ended abruptly:

Welding a pipeline, circa 1930s. (Provincial Archives of Alberta, P1973)

"My father and I each had a team of horses on a buck board fill-ing the ditch. We got about as far as where the gas company had their yard [in Calgary] and the contractors went broke and we didn't get a dime."

Complex monitoring systems keep track of pressures today and quickly react to pipeline leaks, but in the early Turner Valley days the pipelines had to be checked visually, on foot. In the fall of 1929, Lawrence Barker got a job inspecting pipelines as a line-walker in the south end of the oilfield. He walked the main line and the laterals, checking the gas and waterlines. He also walked lines into the Home Oil plant. The first winter the lines were walked 24 hours a day, in three shifts. He walked up to 15 miles a day for 10 years. His brother Syd walked the line to Calgary for seven years and never missed a trip. Breaks occurred in the pipeline a few times each year. Once, a break created a geyser of

gasoline that shot right out of the ground and into a yard where
the homeowner filled up a few barrels with gas.

Alex McKellar walked the pipelines to Calgary and loved the
job: "It was wonderful. I never felt better in my life, and did less."
At least in the warm summer months. Mondays he walked from
the Turner Valley gas plant to the halfway house near the Priddis
corner. Halfway houses were shacks 10 x 12 feet, with a table,
chair, and two bunks. And a lock on the door. In warm months,
the pipeline walkers stocked the small shacks with canned food
and grew flowers and vegetables inside the little fenced-in yard.
Neighbours provided water. Tuesdays, McKeller checked the line
to the refinery in Calgary and the next day he walked lines in the
city. On Wednesday nights he called square dances at two different
dance halls, four dances each. Ma Trainer played the piano at one
hall. On Thursdays he walked a different route, checking the eastern line and staying at the other halfway house. He often helped
the nearby Wiley family break horses or colts, and in exchange,
they fed him supper. On Fridays he walked home to Turner Valley.
Both halfway shacks had stoves in them for cooking and for taking the chill off winter nights. During the cold part of the year the
men took food with them in backpacks, often carrying 50 pounds
or more. The packs included a change of clothes, extra warm
clothing, food, and water. The men also carried snowshoes in the
winter or sometimes a small shovel to dig through the drifts. They
supplied their own mid-height work boots. It took longer to walk
the pipeline in cold weather than in the summer, but they never
got cold. The route was hilly and the exercise kept them warm.
Near the Indian reserve, the men guarded against semi-wild dogs.
Alex shared the pipeline walking work with Adam Blacklock, a
well-known local naturalist. They saw lots of game along the lines.
It was the perfect job for men who loved the outdoors.

It was also work. Pay was $5 per day in the 1920s, less than a full shift at the gas plant in Turner Valley but far more rewarding for the men who appreciated the healthy exercise. At regular internals along the line the walkers checked valves, protected by boxes sunk in the ground. They also checked for leaks in the pipelines, visually inspecting the right-of-way. Alex discovered some small leaks but no large ones. Jim Donnelly, another linewalker, recalled finding a gas leak—indicated by a frozen cone of ground pushed up above the surface. Oil leaks were less spectacular, usually just soaking the ground around the rupture. Linewalkers kept track of pressure levels at each valve, for indirect indications of a leak.

Pipeline leaks wasted very little Turner Valley petroleum compared to the flares. Little did the producers know about the long-term effects of torching the gas as they blasted the precious resource into the air. With environmental concerns still decades in the future, the only concern in the late 1920s was the loss of economic potential. Although they used a small amount for heating and lighting, a bit more for fuelling the steam boilers, in 1929, the operators flared about 158 million cubic feet each day. For a time, the waste was merely a curiosity but the media eventually raised the alarm. In 1939, a *Macleans* magazine article stated that producers were burning off $10 of gas in order to produce $1.20 of oil. Bill Knode, the first chairman of the conservation board, said: "This is a crazy set up. If you let this gas get away, how are you going to raise your oil? And if you can't raise your oil, where will you be?"

While oilfield construction boomed, Royalite's dominant position in the oilfield continued. Its monopoly on the sale of gas to Calgary through the Canadian Western Natural Gas Company remained unchallenged for many years. As capacity for processing gas at the plant in Turner Valley increased, the gas company built another pipeline, in 1928. The new 14-inch line cost $300,000 and boosted capacity from 48 million to 75 million cubic feet per day.

The Big One That Nearly Got Away

Most people know very little about the Turner Valley oilfield. Those that recall the old gas plant that operated until 1985 remember it as a smelly place reeking of hydrogen sulphide, a deadly gas that was a by-product of oil, black gold. Gas, oil, and water lay trapped in the rock formations far below ranching country, and when wells tapped into these pockets, all three tried to escape. Engineers controlled oil development with valves and usually kept the water in the ground. But the gas was harder to control and often came with the oil. With little market for the gas, most producers just burned it and sent the oil and gasoline to market.

As a result, the sky over the oilfield glowed bright orange. Royalite's monopoly on the gas pipeline to Calgary prevented the independents from selling their gas to city consumers, so they routinely flared the gas at each well. Flares at compressors and other production facilities added to the glare. If a pipe sprang a leak, someone lit it with a match to keep if from becoming a dangerous nuisance. No one knows for sure how many flares dotted the oilfield, probably thousands. The light from the flares was so bright that Calgarians read newspapers at night by the glow 45 miles away. Pilots in southern Alberta navigated their airplanes by the huge light that nuzzled up against the mountains.

Nearly everything was visible even on a moonless night. But one flare stood out as the grand-daddy of them all: Hell's Half

Acre. The flare filled a coulee just north of Turner Valley with fire for more than a decade, attracted hoboes during the 1930s, and was a continuous tourist attraction. Windows and doors in the north end of the town of Turner Valley rattled constantly from the way Hell's Half Acre shook the earth. Winter never came to the ground under the flare because it was always baked ceramic-hard, hot, and hostile. Around the flare were scorched little trees, dead grass, and parched ground. At a safer distance, grass, flowers, and weeds grew year round. As a boy, George de Mille went

Dingman Discovery Well, 1914. (Provincial Archives of Alberta, P1301)

with his family on a special trip from Millarville to Turner Valley just to see the famous flare. Two six-inch pipes delivered gas to the coulee. At the edge of the bank the roar was so loud you could not hear the person standing next to you, even when they screamed in your ear. Percy Wray recalled the noise from Hell's Half Acre being so loud that after card games in houses in Turner Valley the players were hoarse from trying to shout over the roar. Tommy Grisdale said ducks got mesmerized by the light from the big flare, flew into the warm air above the roaring blaze and then fell to earth when their wings froze as they flew out into the winter chill. On occasion, he gathered up these fallen birds, warmed them up and released them, apparently unharmed.

Roy Fleiger recalled the method used to light the massive flare. After wrapping a stone in a rag, he soaked it in gasoline. Standing well away from the end of the pipe, upwind, he lit the rag and chucked it towards the end of the pipe. "There would suddenly be a great explosion as the gas ignited, a great roar and a vibration which would rattle the windows all over town."

Alternatives to the Monopoly's Pipeline

Independent producers can perhaps be forgiven for their wasteful habits in the face of Imperial's dominant position when it came to pipelines. For example, in February 1927, Imperial arbitrarily cut the price it paid independent producers for naphtha. In response, a *Western Oil Examiner* editorial called for competition in the refinery trade to combat the high-handed way Imperial treated smaller companies. In August, Regal Oil and Refining Co. Ltd. opened a new Calgary refinery and served the needs of smaller oil companies. The Alberta Pipe Line Company, incorporated that same year with Eric Harvie as president, built a four-inch line from Turner Valley to the new Regal refinery in Calgary. As a result, Royalite's pipeline monopoly ended in 1927. In 1929, Regal Refinery built another four-inch oil pipeline between Turner Valley and Calgary. Its owner, Frank P. Brook of Detroit, thus offered another small alternative in the oil refining sector.

Although competitive pipelines offered some options, Turner Valley production prompted discussion of continental pipelines decades earlier. In the late 1920s and again after the 1936 discovery of crude oil, financiers and promoters dreamed of oil and gas arteries from the isolated oilfield to distant consumers. In late September 1929, gas company officials and members of the Moose Jaw city council visited Turner Valley, investigating the possibility of a gas pipeline from the valley to the Saskatchewan city. The tour entered the oilfield through the north end, where Millarville activity was just beginning. "The first stop was made at 'Hell's Half Acre' where the roar of gas coming from Royalite No. 4 may be heard and the scorching flames belching into the air may be seen and felt. This phenomenal scene along with flames from many other wells greatly impressed the Moose Jaw aldermen who had not the slightest comprehension of the importance of the Turner Valley oil and gas field." Then through the booming Turner Valley village the tour drove, stopping at the plant. "The Royalite scrubbing plant was a point of great interest to the visitors where they were shown by Mr. Yorath and Mr. Coultis the methods in use for the cleansing of gas." They returned to the city through Black Diamond and Okotoks.

That evening Yorath hosted a banquet for the visiting dignitaries at the Palliser Hotel. He warned the Moose Jaw officials that gas supplies in the Turner Valley field did not alone justify a pipeline outside the province, but that "conditions change considerably in the course of a year" and discoveries might be made in Alberta which would warrant the construction of a pipeline to Regina, Saskatoon, and Moose Jaw. Royalite's field supervisor, J.H. Macleod, told the banquet that a new well had just come in that afternoon, adding an additional 27 million cubic feet of gas per day to the valley's flows. "Mayor Pascoe on behalf of members of the Moose Jaw Council, expressed utmost thanks for the great privilege of seeing Turner Valley and viewing the great development that was taking place there."

An article in that September's *High River Times* provided more background. For its part, Imperial Oil was not interested in building a gas pipeline from Turner Valley to Winnipeg for an estimated cost of $50 million. Gas storage seemed too expensive, though the gas company began storing Turner Valley gas in the Bow Island field the next year. Expanding sales to industrial users was not viable due to cheap electricity provided by Calgary Power. Provincial and federal officials, not wanting to discourage development in the booming oilfield, were in a quandary over what to do with the waste gas problem. At the same time, Range Oil and Gas asked Ottawa for permission to build a pipeline and export Alberta's waste gas to the United States from the Rogers-Imperial "gasser" well near the Montana border. If no other economic use could be found for waste gas, the only option would be "limiting of each well to a certain wastage daily, a practice which is followed in the fields in the United States." Turner Valley producers wasted 200 million cubic feet per day in warm months, 150 million cubic feet per day in winter. Compared to California in June of 1929, where the average oil well wasted about 1,000 cubic feet of gas per barrel of oil, Turner Valley producers flared 59,000 cubic feet of gas per of oil, or almost 600 times as much waste.

A solution had to be found and exports seemed to fit the

bill. But pipelines not only link oilfields to markets, they create strong emotional responses in politicians. Range Oil and Gas was only asking for permission to transport waste gas from a single well on the Montana border, but Alberta UFA Premier Greenfield objected, telling Ottawa that the province could not provide "consent to the exportation of natural gas from the Lethbridge or any other field until all the requirements of Alberta are fully protected." Once Ottawa assured Alberta that stringent quotas would govern exports, the province gave its grudging approval to the gas pipeline, but only to export waste gas, and only for this one situation.

In 1929, the *Financial Post* of Toronto hailed Turner Valley as an "Important Asset" and the oilfield was "Spread in British Papers." In 1930, investors from Vancouver visited the field to investigate the prospect of building a pipeline from the valley to the West Coast, and a company with $5 million in British capital received a federal oil charter which included the rights to four million acres in oil leases, including thousands in Turner Valley.

Canadians have never felt at ease unless they know they have a secure supply of gas and oil for their own needs, but Americans comfortably rely on imported petroleum products. Part of the American response is based upon its assumption that Canadian resources will always be available to supply American domestic needs. Western Canadian petroleum history has proved that Turner Valley was always firmly in the grasp of powerful forces much more influential than provincial or federal governments.

Although Turner Valley production alone did not warrant pipeline construction in the late 1920s, the question arose again in the late 1930s. The *Calgary Daily Herald Magazine Section* noted on September 11, 1937: "The British Empire needs oil and Alberta will supply it." After the boom in 1936, residents of

Trenching machine, 1940s. (Glenbow Archives, NA-2719-2)

the south end of Turner Valley were in the kind of mood that let them see the future: "They see the day when Great Britain will turn to Alberta for oil for her navy." Perhaps Turner Valley did not justify the cost of a pipeline in 1937, but regular new finds throughout the area, expanding the oilfield's limits and adding to recoverable estimates, suggested that Turner Valley supplies could be the basis for a pipeline to the West Coast. Oilmen were not a shy lot: "True, they say, the pipeline would cost millions of dollars, but it costs millions of dollars to build battle cruisers, too. And wouldn't a crude oil supply be of more value to Britain in war time than one or two new dreadnaughts?" Turner Valley's amazing oil discovery encouraged speculators to look for other gas and oil fields along the foothills, sending geological field parties out with horses, picks, plane tables, and hopes of finding geological hints or surface seepages that would justify drilling. If they could just find one more field, pipelines to central Canada and the Pacific coast would be viable. If only ...

Closer to home, a December 1938 review of the Alberta petroleum industry in the *Oil Bulletin* noted that although Alberta doubled her oil production in 1938 to 6.5 million barrels of crude oil, the Canadian distribution system was bottlenecked. While Canada imported 30 million barrels in 1938, the Alberta production was prorated, or restricted, due to limited markets. As editor of the Calgary-based oil newspaper, Carl Nickle pleaded with the consumers and politicians of central Canada:

> Wake up, Canada! is the plea of Alberta Oil to the nation. Open your markets in this New Year. Encourage an industry that can pave the way to Security for the Empire, help balance budgets, pull your railroads out of the red, and add hundreds of millions of dollars to the national pocketbook. Look at the record, then try to slumber on!

At a higher level, independent oil company presidents, the conservation board chairman, and provincial politicians all lobbied Ottawa and London, England, to support a pipeline. In May 1939, Robert Benson and Company, investment bankers from England, studied the proposal and concluded that "from a technical point of view construction of the pipeline is thought to present no difficulties" and would cost between £6 and £7 million for a 1,200 mile line from Turner Valley to Port Arthur on the Great Lakes. However, Benson noted that central Canadian refiners had a definite interest in other sources of supply than

Turner Valley, and unless the Canadian government could persuade Canadian refiners to use Canadian supplies instead of imported product, the pipeline project was doomed. Imperial Oil
and British American had both replaced Turner Valley oil in the
Manitoba oil market with American supplies in February 1939,
proving the suspicions held by many Canadians, including Carl
Nickle of the *Oil Bulletin*, that foreign controlled companies were
deciding Canadian oil policy and preventing Canadians from
developing their resources in a way that was appropriate to the
Canadian situation. If Manitoba refiners were using foreign oil, it
was easy to see why central Canadian refiners were importing oil
from the United States and offshore. While nationalists blamed
Ottawa for not taking a stronger hand with the oil companies,
the federal politicians blamed Alberta for its "excessive" royalties. In the end, the Turner Valley pipeline failed and there was
enough blame for everyone to point the finger at other culprits.

Protecting the Resource for the Future

After Alberta gained control over its natural resources in 1930,
it attempted to organize and regulate the booming oilpatch.
Compared to the established coal mining industry, the oil and
gas sector was virtually unregulated, and that's the way most early
oilmen in Alberta wanted it to stay. American oilmen expected
Canada to be just a colder extension of Texas or Oklahoma with
the same wild-west spirit as the early American oilpatch. They
were not amused to find bureaucrats waiting to tell them what
to do. Alberta oilmen did not like being treated as second-class
citizens while Imperial Oil and Royalite set standards, prices, and
operating procedures and blithely violated or ignored laws that
the smaller companies were expected to obey. And Albertans,

Canadians, and even residents of the United States as far away as New York complained about the massive waste of gas in Alberta's biggest oil field.

As the Alberta government responded to the rights and responsibilities that came with ownership of oil and gas, the 1930s slipped away. Attempts by its conservation board to control waste ended up being appealed to the courts by oil companies. Finally, in 1938, it crafted careful legislation that gave power to the conservation board in a way that prevented appeals to the courts. Also in 1938, the government launched a Royal Commission headed by A.A. McGillivray to inquire "into matters connected with Petroleum and Petroleum Products." Although the Royal Commission was an important historical inquiry, Hitler's invasion of Poland in September 1939 ended the pipeline discussion. The Second World War created such a wide demand for oil and gas that the government lifted Turner Valley pre-war production quotas. Overnight, the Canadian West experienced a demand for exploration, production, refining, and distribution to an extent it never dreamed possible.

An Accident Smelled up the System

Demand for gas also proved a powerful conservation incentive. The *High River Times* extolled the virtues of the new resource in an article titled "Blessed Be Gas." It could not say enough about the benefits of safe, cheap natural gas.

> Turner Valley gas enters into 95 percent of the homes of Calgary and into a great majority of the homes in the smaller towns. Through Southern Alberta people are fed and warmed by the power of Turner gas, and

at reasonable cost. The company is indefatigable in
its efforts to serve the public .... Nineteen thousand
customers in Calgary, Lethbridge, Stavely, Parkland,
Nanton, High River, and Okotoks depend on the
Canadian Western Natural Gas Company.

But even though the gas company pumped Turner Valley
gas into the empty Bow Island gas field in the summer to act as
a backup for gas supplies in the winter, on extremely cold winter
nights even Turner Valley's enormous production capacity could
not supply the needs of all the southern Alberta gas customers as
their furnaces struggled to heat poorly insulated homes.

On January 30, 1932, an accident provided a graphic example of southern Alberta's heavy reliance on natural gas. Just as
temperatures plummeted to -30°F, there was an explosion and
fire at the Turner Valley gas plant. Gas reserves at Bow Island
and Foremost could not make up the shortfall. Finally, the gas
company took unprecedented measures. It announced warnings
on Calgary radio stations. Gas company employees went door
to door handing out pamphlets. Then, hoping for the best, the
engineers reluctantly opened the valves and let stinky, raw, hydrogen sulphide-tainted gas flow from Turner Valley to Calgary.
They had no choice. The gas plant could not scrub the deadly
toxin from the sour gas. As a result, southern Alberta gas customers were forced to burn gas that smelled like rotten eggs in
their homes while emergency crews repaired the damaged plant
in Turner Valley.

Although the sour gas gave clients a new appreciation for
living conditions in the Turner Valley oilfield, where residents
routinely burned unscrubbed gas and lived with its hazardous
properties, the brief encounter with the noxious gas also hinted at

another aspect of the relationship between the southern Alberta economy and the oilpatch: unpredictability.

War Solved the Export Pipeline Problem

War gave Turner Valley what it needed, a market. The hostilities frightened many, but Carl Nickle's *Oil Bulletin* saw war as the solution to the independent oilman's problem. Always aligned with locals Carl later represented Calgarians as a member of parliament in Ottawa—he encouraged investors to hang on to their oil stocks in his editorial on September 2, 1939. Although insecurity could cause wary investors to sell, he predicted that there would be an increasing demand for oil worldwide, an escalating oil price, and that the federal government would probably control oil development for the national good. After a period of uncertainty, things would improve: "Your investment in producing royalties can safely be considered 'Gilt-edged.'"

Just as the internal structure of control over the Alberta oil industry was becoming evident, the boom caused by the Second World War distracted disgruntled shareholders and independent oil company owners with an unprecedented period of growth that lasted until the end of the war. Still, Royalite's dominant position in the oilfield continued. On December 11, 1937, its first expansion of the oil pipeline from Turner Valley to Calgary with an additional four-inch line increased capacity from 10,000 to 13,000 barrels per day. On January 1, 1938, Royalite created a pipeline division and Sam Coultis appointed gas plant employee Tom Trotter as superintendent. His duties included building and maintaining all pipelines in the field. On April 23, 1938, Royalite increased the capacity of its oil pipeline to Calgary from 13,000 to 24,000 barrels per day with a new six-inch line.

Although pipeline charges had dropped to 15 cents from a high of 30 cents in 1930, the independent producers requested and received a Royal Commission investigation into the "spread between the field price of crude oil and the wholesale and retail prices." The Alberta government set up the McGillivray Royal Commission on October 12, 1938, and it reported on April 17, 1940. The inquiry found the entire Royalite system to be so closely integrated with Imperial Oil as to make it impossible to distinguish the actual costs of any single part of the exploration, production, refining, or distribution process from the whole. The McGillivray Royal Commission recommended the government have more control over pipelines and make them public utilities. As a result, Alberta gave the public utilities board power over pipelines as common carriers on June 19, 1939. On July 8, 1939, the utilities board took over Royalite's Turner Valley to Calgary pipeline, renamed it Valley Pipeline, and with Sam Coultis as its president in Calgary, began operating the common carrier as a regulated utility to carry oil for all producers. After further investigation, the government reduced the pipeline tariff from 15 cents to less than a penny. When the Royalite pipeline became a public utility, other operators in the field had a better opportunity to market their products.

Pipelines As Utilities

As in other aspects of the Turner Valley oilfield, competition passed out of the pipeline business when the public utilities began transporting oil and gas. But the lines still needed routine maintenance. Some of the techniques reflect today's practices while others provide examples of the attitudes of an earlier time.

Bill McGonigle hired on to help rebuild a pipeline to the

north end during 1950. The pipe needed considerable work due to corrosion, so the workers checked the metal for pitting and welded any repairs. An old gas-powered ditch digger prepared the trench. As they had done for decades, the men wrapped the pipe in burlap, tarred it and lowered it back into the ground. They also added aluminum anode posts every 200 feet along the line to draw electrical current away from the pipeline and ground the system, a new touch technique for reducing corrosion. A caterpillar tractor backfilled after the repair work was completed.

Also in the north end, Bill McIntyre worked for Home Oil. According to him, the company's oil lines were all on the surface until 1955, when it began digging them into the ground. During the winter, the surface lines froze solid, shutting down production completely. Unwilling to wait months until spring came and thawed the lines, the company authorized a most unusual maintenance program. Bill and his men took trucks to the nearby sawmill and loaded them full of sawdust. Along the frozen lines they drove, shovelling the wood chips onto the exposed pipe. "Then you go get buckets of oil and pour on it and light it." Mile after mile of pipeline burned, a red line across the fields and valleys. If the oil still didn't flow, it was back to the sawmill with the trucks for more sawdust to spread on the glowing lines. More oil, wood chips, and oil kept the fire going as long as it took to thaw the sluggish lines.

Construction crews occasionally run into abandoned pipelines but in Turner Valley it was a common occupational hazard for town work crews. Elmer Andersen recalled the early days when the town installed water and sewer lines to each home. The workers often ran into gas or oil lines, and with no maps to indicate their locations, had to rely on oldtimers for advice. They once hit fresh wood right in the middle of Windsor Street, from an oil well basement at an old drill site. Elmer called Royalite and the company came in, dug out the old basement and cemented off the well. Another time the town routed the sewer line around another well on Windsor Street. Royalite employees Bill Powell and Bud Pearson were the only men who knew where the old lines ran, but their knowledge went with them to the grave. Some of the lines in the plant remain unmapped to this day.

Chapter 4

Health and Safety Issues

Unknown pipelines were not the only hazard in the oil-field nor were they the most dangerous. As Pat Tourond found out, things are almost never as they appear in the oil industry. While working at a collection point, a gas heater that was supposed to be flameproof caught fire. It quickly ignited the whole battery. He smothered the fire with snow and rags and in the process got quite badly burned. Due to his dedication to the job the collection battery did not explode, but his story is typical of the kinds of incidents that made the oilpatch a potentially lethal workplace.

Health and safety issues evolved over time. When the Brown brothers came up from the United States to drill some of Turner Valley's first wells in 1913, their attitude towards safety on the rig was typical. Soft cloth caps or hats covered their heads; loose clothing, lace-up boots, and a broad grin of self confidence were their only protection. Whatever the future held, these men could handle it. For decades, the photos show the men with the same work clothes, some with overalls bought at the Chinaman's store in Black Diamond. Safety was a common sense issue for most, but some men even smoked on the job, working with leaking gas pipes that could catch fire or cause explosions.

For many years oilfield work was little different from other construction projects. Early rigs used simple technology familiar to most farmers and homesteaders. As a result, many locals were hired on to work the rigs during slow agricultural seasons and some even learned the more skilled jobs from their co-workers. Anyone with simple carpentry skills could help build a wooden cable-tool rig, install the pulleys and cables necessary to make it work, and assist in other ways around the well. The first gas processing units did little more than strip off the water and liq-

Results of explosion at rig in Turner Valley. (Glenbow Archives, NA-711-95)

uids, a job most men could learn in a few minutes. A strong back meant a job on a pipeline crew or any of the other general construction projects that management assigned to the bull gang.

With time, things became more complex and accidents increased in number and severity. Explosions killed some men, injured others, and left some disabled for life. Fires were common, sometimes burning victims to death or leaving them painfully scarred. Sour gas killed quite a few men, trapping them in well cellars or buildings with deadly hydrogen sulphide. Even the skilled American drillers learned that Canadian high-pressure gas and hydrogen sulphide could paralyze the lungs on contact and kill within a few minutes. Less spectacular incidents killed men too, such as unloading pipe from a truck or falling off a tank or tower.

Workmen's Compensation Board Assessment of Oilpatch Dangers

The Workmen's Compensation Board's insurance premiums give the government's assessment of safety in the oilpatch and comparisons with other occupations. In 1925, for example, the city of Calgary paid 50¢ per $100 of pay to insure its employees with the board, while construction and general building companies paid $1.25. Oil and gas companies paid $1.50 for the same coverage for refinery workers and $3.00 for drillers, the same rate charged to coal mining companies for all their workers. At the beginning of Turner Valley's third boom, in 1937, the rate was 60¢ for city of Calgary employees, $4.00 for construction trades, $2.00 for refineries, $2.25 for drillers, $2.50 for strip coal miners, and $6.00 for underground coal miners. At the peak of Turner Valley production in 1941, the rates rose to 75¢ for city employees, fell to $3.00 for construction trades, dropped to $1.50 for refineries and drillers, stayed at $2.50 for strip coal miners, and rose 50¢ to $6.50 for underground coal miners.

Statistically, only coal miners faced more dangers on the job than oilpatch workers. Underground miners obviously faced hazards unlike any other Alberta workers; when a coal mine exploded or caved in, many men died at once. Drillers probably faced as much danger as miners, but a rig seldom employed more than a handful of men. Even the most disastrous oilfield accidents only resulted in one or two deaths. The same conditions applied to refinery explosions. In the worst year on record before 1945, five men died in an oilpatch population of about 2,400 men while 25 died from 8,600 coal miners. Most years between 1925 and 1945, Turner Valley's busiest period, three or fewer men died in the oilfield workforce that ranged between 500 and 2,400. Mining deaths for the period ranged between 6 and 48 each year for the eight to nine thousand coal miners.

Deaths and Serious Accidents

Overall, the gas plant's safety record was fairly good and less than a handful of men died there. Bert Flathers recalled working on the new plant in 1925, digging holes for footings with a pick and shovel—there were no backhoes in those days. Then one day the foreman sent Bert and another young fellow up a tall tank. The man lifting the platform they were riding jerked the controls and sent them plummeting to the ground. Bert's partner died as a result of his injuries and Bert broke his back, crippling him for life. But given the number of men working at the plant and the lax safety regulations, is it remarkable that there were so few accidents of this type.

The oilfield's record was less admirable. Government accident statistics do not separate oilpatch workers and their accidents well enough from other construction categories to provide a reliable count, but company reports and local and regional newspapers provide a partial record of injuries and deaths caused by this new industry. In 1915, a well caught fire, burning three men badly. The day before, a tinsmith fell from the same rig and broke both ankles. The next year a man badly injured on a rig went to hospital in Calgary. A 1926 explosion blew a separator into hundreds of bits, bruising and injuring several men. The next year five men and two children were burned in an explosion at a well. The children died. In 1928 a derrick burned, sending a man to the Calgary hospital with severe burns to his hands and face.

The last year of the 1920s set a record for bad accidents. A man died and another was injured in two oilfield explosions. Two men died when drilling rods from a rig blowout fell to the ground and crushed them. A load of lumber destined for a rig fell off a truck in Okotoks and crushed a man to death. A man died on a rotary rig after being struck on the head by tools. Another injured employee survived. A man whose arm broke on a rig went to the Calgary hospital. Rock chips imbedded themselves in a man's face as a result of an explosion at a well in November. A driller broke his leg while on duty at a well and went to Calgary so a doctor could set the compound fracture. And in early December, a fire badly burned three men and consumed the engine house and partly damaged the derrick at a well.

On January 6, 1930, an explosion killed a drilling contractor as he attempted to thaw out a frozen water tank at a worksite. Three days later five men suffered bad burns from an explosion at a rig and all had to receive extensive treatment in the Calgary hospital. On March 21 a separator exploded and killed the man working on it. He was apparently trapped by a leg. On April 27 a man suffered a broken leg as the result of an accident when a well blew in. On May 2 an accident at a separator badly injured a man when a valve broke and fractured his jaw in two places. Another man lost three fingers as the result of a rig injury that same day. On October 24 a rig explosion seriously injured two men.

Not every year was as bad as the first of the 1930s. As oilfield work disappeared, the frequency of serious accidents declined. On March 13, 1932, a rig explosion sent a seriously injured rig worker to hospital. On October 29, 1933, four people died and two more suffered serious injury when a truck loaded with pipe collided with a bus and 30-foot lengths of 14-inch pipe speared the passengers. The Royalite annual reports listed 20 "disabling accidents" for 1933 and eight "disabling injuries" for 1934. The local paper reported the death of a man on November 8, 1934. While working on a rig, a steam pipe swung and fractured his skull, killing him instantly.

Accidents increased in number again after the discovery of oil at Turner Valley Royalties No. 1 at the south end of the field in 1936. Royalite reported a total of 37 accidents in 1936, 14 of them including lost time. In once incident, a man lost an eye when a spike flew up into it while he worked on a rig. May 2, 1937, was the last day of work for a man who was crushed to death by a chain on a rotary rig. An accident on August 6, 1937, badly injured a man's finger and forced him to take several days off work. On August 13 a man badly injured on a rig in the oilfield had to go to hospital in High River. On September 4 a man died when a timber fell off a rig and fractured his skull. Finally, on September 24, 1937, a young man received severe cuts to his face when a valve exploded.

In February, 1939, a man fell from a derrick and suffered serious enough internal injuries to require an operation at the

Calgary hospital. A rig worker died as the result of serious injuries on the job in August. In October, two oilfield workers lost digits as a result of accidents: one lost a thumb and the other lost two fingers. Gas killed two men and seriously injured four others in September 1941. In January 1942, a man fell 85 feet from a rig and suffered double leg fractures and serious internal injuries. In July 1942, a man suffered a double fracture when the revolving table and pipe crushed his leg. Another man sustained serious injuries to his head, a broken collarbone, and an injured hip when contact with moving parts threw him across the rig floor. The Royalite annual report for 1943 recorded 64 cases of total temporary disability, two cases of permanent partial disability and two deaths. A man lost both legs below the knee as a result of an accident when a pipe under high-pressure snapped and severed his legs in March 1943. During July, falling casing broke a man's arm and injured his head and torso. In August,

Results of explosion at Royalite #23. (Glenbow Archives, NA-2570-18)

a four-year-old boy drowned in an abandoned well cellar. Gas bubbling up through the water in the cellar probably knocked the child unconscious before he slipped under the water. The company in charge of the well was charged with failing to. protect the site. That same month a spinning rope killed a man working on a rig while casing the well. In October 1943, a man overcome with gas fumes fell from the top of the tank he was gauging and died in hospital as a result of his injuries. That same month an oilfield incident sent a man to hospital with a badly injured left foot. In December 1943, gas fumes killed one man and injured another at a rig accident. On February 7, 1945, a gas leak on a pipeline project killed a man. A collapsing rig on July 28, 1945, killed two men. Finally, on March 8, 1950, a man died while unloading a rig. There were probably more serious injuries and deaths but they did not make the newspaper accounts or official records.

Oilpatch accidents also injured and killed women and children. The gas plant in Turner Valley took safety precautions, but in other parts of the oilfield, families often lived at the worksite. A man in charge of a separator or compressor lived right beside the facility. His wife hung clothes up on a nearby line while the children and pets ran around the wellhead and machinery. Families often visited working rigs for a shower and the drillers' family lived in a shack on the lease. These living conditions became commonplace. But when something exploded, the rig toppled in a high wind or the well blew wild and caught fire, everyone became a potential victim.

Safety Conditions on Rotary Rigs

A rough and tumble attitude contributed to the safety problem too. Contractors drilled many wells in Turner Valley, usually for a set fee per foot of hole. Rotary drilling came into this oilfield in 1925 and replaced cable tool technology by the late 1930s. Speed was a major factor: a cable tool rig took years to drill a well, while a rotary, though more expensive to operate, often completed the job in just a few months.

But many things could, and did, go wrong on rotary wells. Costs varied greatly, depending on many factors. The average American well cost $22,000 to drill in 1937. The same well in California cost $45,000. Canadian wells were not so cheap. Imperial Oil spent an average of $212,000 for each Turner Valley well in 1938. Complex geological formations, importing equipment and supplies from great distances, imported labour and related costs all drove up the average spent on each well. When things went wrong, the American experts were far away, costly to hire, and always worked on a cost-plus basis: a hefty daily rate no matter how long the work took, plus generous expenses.

Wells not only went out of control financially, they sometimes turned into hell on earth. Rotary rigs featured high-powered drilling floors, straining engines, spinning pipe, taught cables, splattering mud, and smelly fumes. Losing a finger or toe, an arm or leg was not uncommon. Exposed moving parts combined with long hours of repetitive labour and mind-numbing fatigue sometimes created deadly situations. A single careless move meant instant injury or death, but workers grew callous to the dangers and flirted with death daily.

Even skilled American drillers often had no experience with two unpredictable and deadly Canadian hazards: high-pressure gas and hydrogen sulphide(H_2S). The extreme pressure that turned Royalite No. 4 into an inferno in 1924 nearly burned the drilling crew to a crisp—a meal break saved their lives. Wellhead pressure was so high that Royalite just let the reservoir push the gas through the processing plant and scrubbers and then through company gas lines to Calgary and other southern Alberta communities. Once, when a gas line broke, the fiercely whipping pipe amputated one man's legs at the knee and only prompt medical attention saved his life. A skilled technician fitted him with artificial legs and he could dance a few months later. The second hazard, hydrogen sulphide, was deadly, until burned, and most gas found after 1924 contained lethal quantities of the foul-smelling toxin.

Gas Plant Safety Conditions and Training

Oilfield safety varied with the workplace as did medical help. Royalite's first aid station overlooked the gas plant in the late 1920s, nestled among a group of buildings, including the main office, geological building, bunk house, and dining room. Royalite hired Dr. Hall as company physician as well as other specialists. In 1928, for example, Joe Milner arrived at the plant's first aid station. Trained in mine safety and first aid at a coal mine in Sheffield, England, Joe came to Canada in 1908 to help at his uncle's mines near Edmonton. He served in the Second World War as a regimental Sergeant–Major with the 7th Field Ambulance Corp. and his experience as an industrial first aid man helped assure safety at the plant.

Royalite sponsored after-hours St. John Ambulance first aid training, in the evenings and on Sunday afternoons. The company paid "the cost of the course for all those who successfully passed their examinations" and the certificates were good for five years. In addition to the many men with first aid training, Dr. Harry Lander and Dr. David Lander attended serious accidents promptly: "They were very faithful people. They would go out at any time of the day or night." There were also weekly safety meetings which lasted 15 to 20 minutes, recalled Ruth Pearson, with good attendance. Jim Donnelly said the men reviewed safety procedures for up to an hour each week. They tested and used equipment and brushed up on fire-fighting training. Some fire extinguishers had water in them though the ones used on oil fires contained foam.

The booming south end in the 1930s was not as well organized. Gerry Shultz recalled a fairly lax attitude towards safety training when he started on rigs for Drilling Contractors and general construction for Anglo-Canadian. No hardhats, no first aid courses, just drilling and building to keep up with the incredible demand for new wells and related production and distribution facilities.

Fred Cowling recalled the first hardhats—big cumbersome tin monsters, with large brims that banged into everything. Lawrence Watrin, a rancher, Calgary Stampede rodeo legend, and stuntman for many Hollywood movies shot in the Alberta foothills, said he started using hardhats on drilling rigs in about 1938 or 1940. By the end of the Second World War most oilfield workers used them regularly.

Asbestos was another health hazard. Ralph Steen "did an awful lot of insulation work." Pipes covered in asbestos often needed repairs. "Handling that asbestos—we'd take it and pulverize it, hammer it. We used to go into the old fire hall, and you never thought anything about it, but the air would just be full of particles of asbestos." He did not think it bothered his lungs even though he smoked for many years. "We'd be inside the shop and you'd take a big wooden mallet and beat it and pulverize it because it all had to be made up fine. After you got it pulverized then you'd moisten it, and if there were holes in the insulation in the pipes, then you'd have a little trowel and trowel it in, like a paste. About an inch think—we'd patch them. Then we used to get unbleached shirting, in bolts from Montreal, a good grade of cotton. We made a flour and glue paste, put in a steam hose and then cook that paste. Then you'd put the cloth round the pipe and paint it with a paint brush and that stuff would just shrink on there. Then they'd paint it with aluminum paint afterwards and it would last for years on there—it was a better grade than what the insulation come out with originally."

Weeds were a nuisance at the plant and workers apparently controlled them in several ways. Elmer Andersen said the plant sometimes hired high school boys to chop the weeds off at ground level with hoes, stack them outside the fence, and set fire to the piles. Ernie Carter worked on the crew that cut the weeds by hand, and Ralph Steen said Royalite also killed weeds by hacking them off with hoes and then spraying raw oil and cleanings from

Bridge at Turner Valley Gas Plant, 1920s. (Glenbow Archives, PA-2297-111)

the tanks on the ground to stunt further growth. Alex McKellar worked on bull gangs but did not remember the plant applying any chemicals to the weeds, suggesting instead that the "stink around there kept the weeds killed."

Deadly Hydrogen Sulphide

The "stink" was sour gas, of course, and hydrogen sulphide probably cost more lives than anything else in the oilfield. Ernie Carter worked at the plant and recalled frequent lectures on safety. "The company was very safety conscious." But he still had accidents. "I got gassed and fell off a tank a few times. I probably should have been wearing a gas mask and didn't. Too lazy, too much trouble." It was a common attitude. "Deaths were quite common as gas of any kind was toxic—just excludes the oxygen. If you get into it too long, you're in trouble."

Hydrogen sulphide was almost everywhere. Although the 1914 discovery well was "sweet" or contained almost no sulphur, all wells drilled in the 1920s and later contained deadly amounts of sour gas. Gas company customers burned scrubbed gas throughout southern Alberta but Turner Valley residents lived with sour gas in their homes for a generation. Ralph Steen recalled working in the compressor plant where there was enough stray hydrogen sulphide floating around that any food left in the building became nearly inedible by mealtime. Some men ate the food anyhow, probably unaware of the fouled taste because of their own exposure to the H_2S. Royalite had a lunch house at the plant, separate from the processing buildings, and food stored there tasted better.

A sense of bravado caused some men to claim they developed immunity to H_2S, but in fact, tolerance for the toxic substance decreases with exposure. Ralph Steen lost much of his sense of smell, probably due to continual exposure to sour gas. Eric Mulder, a knowledgeable engineer, claimed the H_2S ratio in the gas was 500 grains per hundred cubic feet in the centre, 3,500 in the northern end, and 2,500 at the southern end of the field. Even incredibly small amounts of the toxic substance knocked out a person's sense of smell, a bit more paralyzed the lungs, and unless someone rescued the incapacitated person quickly, the victim was dead within minutes.

And it wasn't just enough to know that sour gas was deadly. Sulphur corrodes steel quickly, making it brittle. Although the pipe might look solid from the outside, it could be almost rusted away inside and rupture at the slightest touch. Or gas pressure alone could create a leak. The plant painted sour gas lines a bright yellow as a warning. Red Kennedy taught his employees to use their heads first and their hands second when dealing with hydrogen sulphide.

Even so, men grew accustomed to working with deadly gas and grew careless or complacent. By the late 1930s, all rigs had gas masks but the men considered them a nuisance and refused to wear them. A young Black Diamond man, Kevin Cassidy, died on the Major No. 3 well in 1941 at the north end of the oilfield when sour gas came up the well and overcame him. The crew scrambled to close the rams and stop the sour gas but while fighting to control the well, two other men also succumbed to the sour gas and died.

Drilling deaths were unpredictable but the men at the gas plant knew they were working with sour gas. In the 1940s, hydrogen sulphide killed operator Gus Olsen when he ran into the scrubbing plant to restart the fans after a power failure. Sour gas paralyzed his lungs as soon as he entered the building and he fell to the floor. Two other men went in to save him and they also collapsed. Rescuers pulled all three out and revived the last two. After the fatality, the company moved the switches outside the building so that if the fans quit again, the men would not be exposed to the sour gas in order to restart the motors.

Art Martin died at the plant when a vessel froze up, cracked and exposed him to gas. The vessel was not currently in use, near the scrubbing plant. Hydrogen sulphide accumulated in the valve and leaked out into the air. It was an unfortunate accident that need not have happened. Eleven others were checked out at the hospital as a result of the same accident that killed Martin.

Even the relative safety of the open field could be deceiving. Routine tasks like walking pipelines and gauging tanks could turn deadly without warning. The north end had gas concentrations as high as 15%. Several men passed out in tanks and had to spend time in hospital. Bill McIntyre recalled one particularly sad accident: "A young lad was visiting one of the operators and one of the operators made a mistake and he went up to gauge the tank and never came back again."

Carelessness and a lack of understanding of the dangers inherent in the processing of gas caused most accidents. Eric Mulder once went up to gauge a tank at a well. Unaware of the sulphur content, he was less careful than wise. The separator dumped its oil into the tank and gas burped out of the top of the tank. Overcome by the hydrogen sulphide, he fell "spread-eagled" on top of the tank and awoke later, much later.

Gas burps while drilling, accumulations in low spots, sour gas in pits or tanks, and many other predictable hazards faced the men every day. In the early days, rescuers just held their breath and ran in to drag out a man if he fell down from exposure to hydrogen sulphide. As Bill Lockhart learned about the danger of sour gas, he did not let any of his men go into the cellar of a well without a rope attached to their waist in case they were overcome. Once exposed to sour gas, men succumbed more easily on subsequent exposures. Lockhart remembered being partly gassed once but he rolled away from it. "One fellow on my crew, we pulled him out, and he said he could hear us talking but he couldn't answer us. But he sure knew what we were talking about. That's the way it hit him."

Pat Tourond worked with hydrogen sulphide for years and got gassed four or five times. "All of a sudden, you had bells in your ears and you were down on the ground. So you'd wake up, you'd find yourself laying, looking at the stars. Your head would start ringing and then you'd get out of the gas, your legs are like rubber and then down you went. Couldn't move. Someone had to drag you out." In one case a man was unconscious five or six hours but in most circumstances those affected came back in a few minutes. Turner Valley was sour compared with other fields. "The gas was absolutely different in Swan Hills, it was a sweet gas. All you got was a glorified drunk out of it."

Prevention included using gas masks, if you could stand the ridicule of fellow workers. Some had canisters on them, often just equipment left over from the war. Fred Cowling and Bill McIntyre both recalled using face masks connected to a hose and a crank box that supplied a positive pressure of fresh air. They used this system when cleaning out oil storage tanks.

In spite of the best efforts to avoid H_2S, it sometimes caught up with the men after hours, at home. Very small concentrations of gas built up in the liquid of the eye. Pat Tourond experienced "gassed eyes" often but was usually better by the next morning. His eyes usually started watering right away. Others said it felt like someone threw gravel in their eyes, which became red and inflamed. Red Kennedy said: "It's like thousands of needles in your eyes, it's painful." Bill McGonigle recalled that gassed eyes created blue circles around the lights in the house. It sometimes took two or three days to go away, but most men remembered being able to go back to work on the next shift. Bill just washed his eyes out with water or put in drops that the doctors gave him.

Druggist Joe Korczynski said the physicians handed out castor oil drops and cocaine drops for the pain caused by gassed eyes. Fred Cowling often put grated potato on his eyes when they hurt, and the potatoes turned black as the sulphur soaked into the cure. His eyes were bloodshot for a few days after being gassed. Geoff Andrews recalled a bath of boracic acid worked

(Provincial Archives of Alberta, P2618)

well for gassed eyes. Les Lake came home a few times with gassed eyes and his wife, Gladys, put wet tea bags on each eye until the sting went away. Bill McGonigle and his mother both experienced gassed eyes—their homes burned unprocessed gas until the late 1930s. They subscribed to the wet tea-leaf solution as a cure and felt relief after 8 to 10 hours.

Bill McIntyre worked with sour gas for years. It only knocked him out twice but it brought him to his knees many times. It might not have been laughing gas, but it caused some situations that had humorous aspects. Bill passed out once and it took a while for him to regain his senses. His wife came to his side, comforting him, doing what she could to make sure he came back to the land of the living. Finally, one guy said: "He's not even dead and you are already coming over to get his wallet!"

Minor Safety Considerations

Other aspects of plant safety were less serious, though potentially dangerous. Many employees smoked, and although officially prohibited from doing so on the job, some men lit up cigarettes inside the plant. The only places the plant allowed the men to smoke were at the lunch room, the water pumphouse, and the steam plant. Ever-present gas in the rest of the plant made smoking a very dangerous proposition.

The ever-present sulphur in the air was sometimes a problem. Although the men wore eye protection while bagging the powdered sulphur, Jim Donnelly got sore eyes from the fine dust at the plant. The sulphur dust also wafted its way outside the plant, through the fence and onto the nearby parking lot at the swimming pool. Elmer Andersen remembered that car exhaust sometimes started fires at the swimming pool by the plant.

Sulphur powder sometimes ignited, but the fires never amounted to much—the caretaker at the swimming pool quickly put them out with a water hose.

After fire consumed the first gas plant in 1920, the rebuilt facility used steel structures to minimize future problems. Jim McInnis recalled very few fires at the plant, spread out as it was to prevent even a small flame from getting out of control. They used foamite fire extinguishers when he worked at the plant. Fred Cowling remembered pop valves—relief valves catching on fire during lightning storms. Brave workers then climbed up the pipes and batted out the flames with wet gunny sacks.

In the nearby machine shop, operators were perhaps not as cautious as they should have been in the early years. Geoff Andrews began his apprenticeship there in 1936 and eventually became a lathe operator. The men wore goggles when working on the grindstone but did not wear them at the lathe. As a result, the lathe operators sometimes got metal filings in their eyes. When they did, another worker used a small tool with a loop of fishing line sticking out of the end to extract the filing from the eyeball.

Although there were few visible moving parts in the gas plant, it made an incredible amount of noise. Night and day it hummed and howled. Ear plugs and ear muffs helped control the noise, but many men lost their hearing early in life as the result of their careers at the plant. Others recalled a buildup of wax in their ears, perhaps as nature's own protection. But Gladys Lake remembered another side to the roar: her husband Les Lake worked in many capacities at the plant and knew the sounds intimately: "Les just grew up with the plant. He could listen to the plant and know what was wrong."

That which did not kill was probably not always good for

the survivors. Before Royalite bought the propane plant and moved it to the plant site in 1952, it operated in a squatters' community called Cuffling Flats, just upstream. According to Lawrence Barker, an accident at the propane plant one summer ruined all the gardens in Cuffling Flats—gassing them and killing their crops.

Unions and the Industrial Council

Imperial's paternalistic attitude also applied to labour organizations in the oilfield and particularly at the gas plant. As Turner Valley oldtimer Geoff Andrews recalled, unions could not organize rig workers due to the instability of the work. Drilling was feast and famine: when in high demand, drillers could make a good wage and didn't need a union to protect their wages; when there were no drilling jobs, a union was powerless. Unions had a better chance organizing at more stable workplaces, such as refineries. But the Turner Valley story has its own twists and turns.

Oilfield folklore suggests that unions were not necessary due to the independent nature of employees and the kind consideration offered by companies. However, Turner Valley's largest employer had one attitude to labour organizations in the valley and another elsewhere. According to the *Imperial Oil Review*, by the beginning of 1925 company-controlled unions, called joint industrial councils, were in place in almost all its major production facilities. The monthly magazine noted that these organizations "would send men about their work with the calm consciousness that so long as the industry flourished their welfare was safe. All wage adjustments [were] made in [industrial] council, subject to the approval of the Directors." Curiously, there was no joint industrial council at Turner Valley at that time.

Unions did try to get into the oilfield. The Calgary Stationary Engineer's union prosecuted six engineers for working without licenses in the oilfield in 1914. Five of these men were convicted, one was acquitted, and sixteen more were considered as possible cases. In 1929 the International Union of Operating Engineers gave a charter to a Local 957 at Turner Valley. It boasted 100 members and hoped to attract the remainder of the 300 engineers who worked in the valley. The *Calgary Herald* reported 29 signatures on the incorporation documents and that regular meetings occurred every second Tuesday of the month. The union lasted until the early 1930s, when its weekly advertisement in the local Turner Valley newspaper disappeared along with the union itself as the depression shut down almost all oilfield activity.

Supply room at Seismic Service Supply, c. 1950. (Provincial Archives of Alberta, P3253)

While Calgary boasted a cantankerous newspaper called *The Eyeopener* and its vociferous editor Bob Edwards, Turner Valley had its equivalent in *The Flare* and its proprietor, Barney Halpin. As a commentator over Turner Valley's largest boom, Halpin reported the oilfield news and passed judgement on almost every event of the day, far and near. Like his infamous Calgary counterpart, Barney knew how to drink. He was a good writer too, and, according to Freda McArthur, "was in trouble a lot." Barney also wrote many poems criticizing the Social Credit government. He kept track of the pulse of the community and wrote a regular column that Lawrence Barker recalled "was about people around here, and though he didn't mention names, the things that he told about, you could figure it out." The word "clever" appeared often when people talked about Barney and local school principal Gordon Minue said that he was "to a certain extent, a character." Geoff Andrews recalled that Barney once reported that a forest fire was "fought by 36 white men, two Indians and Percy Wray." RCMP officer "Bus" Rivett sponsored local sports teams and considered Barney a jovial man. As the editor of the newspaper, Barney wrote up the sporting events of the local boys.

There was little Barney would not tackle. In September 1937 his paper carried an editorial calling for an association to protect the workers. The producers had organized their own protective association in 1926, so he thought a local labour organization should balance the issue. It could educate members on the latest technology and persuade local companies and the governments to improve conditions in the oilfield. He reasoned that a local union would make better sense than an outside organization which might hinder development.

When no indigenous union sprang up in 1937 or 1938,

two car loads of welders drove out from Calgary to start a local chapter of the welders' union in April 1939. *The Flare* noted that oilfield men wanted "more protection from the government for men holding papers but no good was discerned by forming a union." Without local support, the specialized welders' union had no chance of gaining a foothold in the Turner Valley oilfield.

The next union drive came during the Second World War. In July 1942, *The Flare* announced that Jim Conroy of the Canadian Congress of Labour was coming to the oilfield. He intended to form a union with engineers and welders as founding members. The article invited engineers, welders, drillers, roughnecks, and others to the founding meeting at the Black Diamond hall. The article concluded: "It is to the advantage of all oil workers to attend the meeting next Monday." Fifteen men attended the first meeting of Local No. 1 of the Oilfield Engineers and Affiliated Workers of Alberta and 40 engineers and welders quickly joined the union. Wages were fair, but firing without just cause was one reason for this union. More than 100 men were members by September, paying $2 monthly dues. Men joined from every major oil company and *The Flare* added that "there [was] no reason why this Union should not become a powerful factor for the betterment of working conditions in the field."

As many oldtimers recalled, there was not a chance that the union would "become a powerful factor" in the oilfield because Royalite and Imperial Oil did not want unions in their facilities. Overnight, a joint industrial council appeared at the gas plant. Although the *Royalite Annual Report* claimed the men were not interested in an industrial council in early 1943, by December they were involved in the council. Royalite employees probably did not want to join the company union earlier, since the council always included more management representatives than workers.

The company forced a council on the workers when the union threatened to take over the Turner Valley oilfield.

The relationship between workers and managers at the gas plant changed over time, and their recollections help explain the evolution. In the earliest days men like Sam Coultis, plant construction supervisor and manager, taught unskilled men all aspects of the trade. A relatively small group of men solved technical and workplace problems together, with Sam acting as a benevolent commander. Many of his early employees became managers too, some advancing within Royalite to high positions. In the 1920s, a few dozen managers and employees lived within walking distance of the plant. Their families socialized, hunted and fished together, played golf and hockey.

During the Depression, Royalite helped the unemployed with food hampers, spread out the work as much as possible, and even sidelined its mechanized ditch-digger in order to make work for men with picks and shovels. When the oilfield boomed again, thousands of men flocked into the oilfield and found jobs. Drillers, pipeline workers, construction crews, plant operators, office workers, and many others swelled the ranks of the largest employer. Managers still knew the men quite well, often curling with them after work and then going for a swim at the heated outdoor pool. But during this boom the ranks of managers swelled the community called Snob Hill and class divisions, always somewhat evident, widened between the well-to-do and the less fortunate.

Jim McInnis recalled these times and the place the Industrial Council played in social order at the plant. "One of the supervisors told me, 'You know what you're gonna get, you're just going to get what the union gets in Ontario. There's no use in us discussing wages.' And that's what we got." Ruth Pearson said the Industrial Council met once a month in Calgary. The biggest issue was wages. "The company always discussed everything with the members of the Industrial Council. They came to an agreement." Ruth was a secretary and recalled that office staff were excluded from the Industrial Council. Ruth later married a manager. Frank Briggs thought the Council was good. His wife, Melvina, recalled: "He said that no one needed to be on a union as long as they were treated as well as they were treated by this company. I felt the same way. I felt they were really great."

Ralph Steen also appreciated the Industrial Council. He liked it much better than working under a union in a Royalite plant in British Columbia. While working at the Kamloops refinery, the Oil and Chemical Workers Union went out on strike. Ralph lost $1,000 in wages since the union only paid $10 a week for strike pay. In Turner Valley, he felt like Royalite treated him as part of the family. When he fell sick with a bleeding ulcer, Royalite paid for the blood. When he tried to repay the company, someone representing Royalite, said "No way, if we can't do that for one of our employees." He felt part of a big family while he worked under the Industrial Council in Turner Valley.

As the plant grew larger, it imported managers from other operations. George de Mille recalled, "A lot of them were originally Calgary people and they looked upon it as being sort of a purgatory." They put in time until they could apply for a transfer elsewhere. The sense of friendship common in early years disappeared with time, and animosity crept in. Maurice Edwards found the Industrial Council powerless to effect change and a less benevolent attitude developed as time passed. When he asked for a regular daytime job instead of shift work, the manager demoted him to No. 1 maintenance, the lowest paid job in the plant. He knew the company had a policy that any man who had operated for 50 percent or more of his time was entitled to be paid as

though he was an operator, regardless of his position. When he
mentioned his complaint to the representative on the Industrial
Council, the company ignored his case. His demotion lasted four
years. Once the manager moved to Saskatchewan, the new superintendent promoted Maurice to a higher paying job.

Oilfield wages were good to excellent, often better than for
other work available at the time. In 1929, for example, labour-
ers made $5 per day as did men who worked on the separator, a
primitive device for stripping liquids from wet gas. The man who
operated the mechanized ditcher took home $6 per day. Men
who took manually digging pipelines worked for a contract rate
of 4¢ per foot of trench. When the hard times came in the early
1930s, wages dipped, and only rebounded to late 1920s levels
after 1936. Work was steady at the gas plant and operators took
home $110 per month in 1934. Ernie Carter worked for Royalite
as a trench digger, installing pipelines by hand for 55¢ per hour
in 1937. When drilling boomed again after 1936, wages on the
rigs steadied. Roustabouts, floormen, and other unskilled labour-
ers got $5.50 to $5.75 per day. Cathead men and derrick men
got $6.75 per day and drillers took home $14 per day. An Alberta
government survey found that oilfield workers averaged $1,531
in 1938, or more than three times the $431 farm labourers made
the same year.

In recognized trades there was a more formal system of pay
increments. Royalite operated a machine shop beginning in the
late 1930s. Welders and many other skilled tradesmen worked
in the shop. As a machinist apprentice at the plant, Ed Andrews
started in 1936 at a wage of 30¢ per hour that increased after 18
months to 40¢ and to 55¢ per hour after another 15 months. In
1939, newly married, he hired on as a third-class machinist for
70¢ an hour.

Chapter 5

Housing and Living Conditions

A job was one thing, but finding a place to live in the early oilfield was another. Royalite's operations in Turner Valley boomed as a result of its 1924 discovery. Before the boom, there was relatively little activity along Sheep Creek. Sam Coultis lived in a solitary white frame house on the south side of the river, and a few of his workmen squatted in shacks on the floodplain below his home. They called their squatters' village Poverty Flats. Bill Herron lived upstream by a rock cut and operated his Okalta Oils company from a modest home. A small building north of the Royalite plant served as Royalite's first office and a handful of small homes and a school sat further north. North of the community a few independent wells drilled for oil, each with a few tents or shacks for their workers. A road, little more than a track, snaked along the north side of Sheep Creek to Black Diamond and the nearest store.

By the late 1920s many local farmers and ranchers worked wage jobs on oilfield construction crews and hundreds of other people flocked to the valley from all over the west, looking for work. Likely as not, there was a job of some sort for nearly everyone who followed the light of the flares on the horizon. There were skilled jobs for road and rig builders, drillers (both cable tool and rotary) welders, machinists, boiler operators, gasfitters, and anyone else with even modest mechanical talents. For the strong back and untrained mind there was work digging pipeline trenches, cutting weeds in the plant yard, digging holes for footings, cutting brush for new roads, digging waterwells and outhouse holes, moving gravel with team and wagon from the riverbed to the plant or low spots in the roads, laying waterline for the steam boilers, and doing numerous other brutal, backbreaking jobs. Royalite paid for most of this work.

There was literally no place to stay in the oilfield, no hotels, motels, rooming houses, or even extra buildings at nearby farms. As drilling boomed and additions to the plant continued without end, demand for housing ballooned. Royalite provided room and board for some of its workers. Just northwest of the plant, the company built bunkhouses for single men and the housing became known as "The Batch." "The Batch" was a group of buildings connected together east across the road from the plant office. Each man had a small room of his own, a bed with springs and a mattress, a chair and table as well as a small stove. The company supplied bedding. A janitor changed the sheets each week and cleaned the central bathroom and showers. The company dining room served meals round the clock to the drilling crews. The bull gang ate breakfast and supper at the dining room and took along lunches in old lard pails for the mid-day meal. Roy Flieger recalled: "We had good cooks and the fare was the best that could be found anywhere." Bill Lockhart remembered as many as 175 men eating at one time in the Royalite dining room. Mrs. Falardo cooked for Royalite. The company supplied these amenities to its men at a cost of $1.50 per day in the late 1920s—wages ranged from $5 a day for bull gang members to a high of $14 per day for senior men on drilling crews. When the boom burst in the early 1930s, "The Batch" closed for a few years but opened again when things got busy in the late 1930s. When these men moved into their own housing "The Batch" became a place for women to live who came to the oilfield to work in the plant office. Before the war, all the clerks and secretaries working for Royalite were men.

Various other boarding and rooming houses popped up during the 1930s, operated by Mrs. Yost, Mrs. Watchhorn and others. A building called the Log Cabin sat near the centre of town in Turner Valley and served many roles, including a rooming house. Built by local craftsmen using lumber from the forests to the west, it became the social centre for the oilfield. At first it offered meals on the main floor and a place for single men to bunk upstairs in one large room. With time, the owners created a series of suites. When the Donnelly family lived there, they held dances and charged 25¢ per head to raise money for the Social Credit political party. The Donnellys also provided room and board for single men and for workers who returned home on the weekends. When Fred Sargeant operated it in 1942, he charged $1.25 per day for room and board.

Alberta's First Scheduled Air Shuttle

Beginning in August 1929, a Rutledge Air Service plane lifted off from the airfield in northeast Calgary twice each day. Once airborne, the American Eagle biplane did not turn east towards Regina, Winnipeg, and Toronto. It did not set its wings for

Stinson Detroiter at High River airport, 1930s. (Glenbow Archives, NA-2097-44)

Edmonton to the north or head west to Vancouver. Instead, the pilot of Alberta's first regularly scheduled provincial air shuttle flew southwest towards the mountains. After 20 minutes in the air, the plane landed on the grass airstrip in downtown Turner Valley. The morning flight returned to Calgary at 9:45 A.M., but the afternoon flight waited until 7 P.M. to "allow tourists to make a tour of the oil field."

And what an oilfield it was. By 1929, Turner Valley was the largest oilfield in the British Commonwealth. It had two booming communities, incorporated as Black Diamond and Turner Valley. They boasted streetlights, policemen, dogcatchers, banks, telephones, doctors, lawyers, dentists, and even a small hospital. Pool halls, gambling houses, prostitutes, shacks and slums were part of the mix in the numerous settlements that appeared overnight. Only Black Diamond and Turner Valley had bylaws to create some sort of social order.

In these early days, no laws restricted the natural gas industry in the Valley. The boom meant jobs for everyone, skilled or not, free natural gas to heat homes and provide light, and free or cheap gasoline for every car and truck. The land of plenty grew quickly, often unaware of the problems it was creating for itself and future Albertans. For a time, no one cared. During this second Turner Valley boom, a multinational oil company and independents exploited the natural resources in a careless manner, wasting more resource than they delivered to market. They followed senseless development habits similar to those in early American oilfields and defied government agencies that tried to control their activities. As a result, much of the potential of the Turner Valley field was wasted in the 1920s and 1930s. One government estimate claimed that producers flared off as much as half of the total recoverable gas in the field between 1924 and 1930.

At 7 p.m. the Eagle biplane taxied to the north end of the grass airstrip in downtown Turner Valley—right across from the shops on Main Street! With a guttural roar the air-cooled piston engine pulled the airplane through the evening air and it lifted off over an oilfield community full of hope for a bright future. Above the gas plant the plane banked and turned northeast, headed for Calgary. Hell's Half Acre screamed in its earthen cage below, howling loud enough to be heard by the pilot and his passengers. Smaller flares dotted the early evening landscape. Children playing at the squatters settlements stopped to watch the plane pass overhead. As the largest oilfield in Canada, Turner Valley was proud of its place on the map. The future looked fine.

Sidestepping the Great Depression

And for a time, the oilfield held out against the dark years of the

1930s. Black Diamond and Turner Valley apparently snubbed the economic downturn. Recently incorporated as villages, they continued growing; indeed, they burst at the seams. Residents authorized streetlights, fire protection services, sidewalks, and many other services. They gave their streets plain names like Main Street and grandiose ones like Frontenac Avenue, Royal Avenue, and Sunset Boulevard. Restaurants served meals around the clock to the 2,000 men who worked on 90 or more rigs.

The oilfield's most famous hotel opened in 1930 and became an instant legend: at the Black Diamond Hotel bar, even the women fought. "Bud" Widney recalled it as the place where beer taps began pouring at 7 A.M. and where fights broke out all the time because "there was nobody to stop you." On the odd occasion when the Alberta Provincial Police or the RCMP showed up, the fights stopped, temporarily. The hotel was also part of the informal health care system in the oilfield—many a man went to the bar for an anaesthetic before going to the doctor. Don Coultis lost both index fingers in an accident on a drilling rig. After bandaging his hands, the crew took him to the bar for quite a few beers. Then it was upstairs to the doctor's office to repair the damage.

For decades the hotel at the crossroads in downtown Black Diamond was harmless enough, though a local joke hinted at the excesses sometimes experienced in the first legal drinking establishment in the oilfield:

Waiter: Would you like anything to drink?
Customer: Yes, bring me some ale.
Waiter: Pale, sir?
Customer: Just a glass will do.

But just a little was not enough for most who visited the Black Diamond bar or for other oilfield residents. They spent money like there was no tomorrow.

Mary Gooding reported on local conditions as a stringer for the *Calgary Herald* during the boom times. "Much water has run down the bed of the old Sheep River since gay splotches of dande-lions were uprooted among the willow bushes to make way for the tar paper shacks that were crowded into every available space."

Fire

Then disaster struck. Fire broke out on Monday morning, April 20, 1931, and by noon there was little left of the business section of Turner Valley. The Royal Cafe stood as did Roche's Drugstore but everything else was in ashes. The picture taken from a rig

Garbage disposal system in Little Chicago, also called Royalties. (Glenbow Archives, NA-2895-16)

across the street shows people milling about, sorting through the rubble for anything to salvage. In the street, a fire extinguisher. A lone fire wagon stands useless by the smouldering ruins of a store. Even the wooden sidewalk burned. For two blocks almost everything was reduced to embers. People's hopes and dreams, lifelong savings invested in businesses—all was gone. Many shop owners lived in accommodations behind or above their stores. If lucky, they saved a few things from the blaze, but the fire consumed their livelihoods and their homes.

Behind the gaudy veneer of the exaggerated storefronts and excited activity, oilfield life was less than glamorous. What the fire revealed was a village of shacks. The tiny houses had no siding, no insulation, no protection against fire. Sheds housed chickens, pigs, and other animals. Dogs and cats wandered about. Gas lines snaked through back alleys, on the surface, leaking gas laced with dangerous hydrogen sulphide. Flares got rid of it with only a stinky smell, but if it sank into a low spot, it could kill anyone who inhaled the deadly gas. Outhouses dotted backyards, squished between the shacks and the back alley. In the background, wooden rigs, once testimony to a booming town, sat idle and abandoned. Many wells were dry holes. The 22 power poles that took electricity up grandly named Sunset Boulevard were mostly for show; Calgary Power turned off the electricity for non-payment. And as always, a flare blasted away above the scrub, the symbol of the enormous waste of gas that reduced the potential recoverable oil and gas from the oilfield.

Bankrupt!

The residents of Black Diamond and Turner Valley have always had their differences—they still do, but in 1931 the councillors for both villages climbed into one car and headed north. In Edmonton they met the officials of the provincial municipal affairs department. The boom had gone bust. The local politicians were no longer capable of running the oilfield communities, and so they declared bankruptcy. Fires, floods, layoffs, the masses of unemployed, and the general shutdown in the oilpatch had soured the boom. The councillors turned the financial records over to the provincial government. Like many small incorporated communities in Alberta in the early 1930s, the oilfield villages officially declared bankruptcy and threw themselves on the mercy of a poor provincial government. Almost overnight the glowing promise of the flares and derricks turned into a government headache. Records show that until the villages regained self-sufficiency in the mid-1940s, provincial taxpayers paid for many local services, including: fire protection, indigent relief for the unemployed, street repairs, mothers' allowances, doctors' bills, and other health care costs including medicine and hospital bills, child welfare expenses, old age pensions, cemetery costs, waterworks and sanitation expenses, office repair bills, sidewalk and street lighting costs, skating rink expenses, as well as giving payments to the Turner Valley Women's Institute and the Blind Institute.

The Department of Municipal Affairs hired Percy Wray as secretary-treasurer for the Turner Valley community for $25 per month, later giving him the same job in Black Diamond for an additional $35 per month. No one recalled the details of life in these tough times better than Percy. With many unemployed, Turner Valley did what it could to help out its residents. The towns paid for lumber, for example, and the residents held a building bee to make sidewalks. Percy personally visited the Calgary hospitals on behalf of oilfield residents because those unable to pay for medical help simply charged their bills to the village. With cap in hand, Percy negotiated a discount on outstanding bills.

The provincial government was tight during the early 1930s. Taxpayers who fell behind on their bills could work off their debts with road work, wielding a pick and shovel. The government handed out small amounts of emergency cash to the poor and unemployed. When times got really tight and starvation loomed, Royalite made up food hampers. Tom Trotter, a manager at the gas plant, delivered food to the unemployed as part of his job. Another time Royalite gave its horse wrangler, Sandy McNabb, some cash and sent him to a local ranch. There he and a few of the hungry unemployed bought a cow, butchered it, and distributed the beef to needy families.

People managed, somehow. Many owned their tiny shacks, but few owned land. Some squatted while others rented a small lot from Francis Wurstemberger for $3 per month. When the economy improved, he sold lots for $10 per foot of frontage. Most lots were 33.3 feet wide. There were two water men in town, delivering door to door with horse and wagon for 5¢ per pail or 25¢ for a barrel. They filled their tanks at a spring by the river and passed through the streets every day. One tap downtown provided free water to people willing to carry it home. When the spring floods drenched the countryside, the Turner Valley village became a soggy mess. Outhouse pits overflowed and polluted water poured into the water wells. In Black Diamond, the flooding river polluted the wells. At one point in the early 1930s, all the water in both villages was deemed unfit for human consumption.

Floods, Dumps and Shacks

Although spring floods threatened oilfield residents many times, the deluges in the early 1930s were memorable. Squatters' settlements in the river's floodplain suffered most. Residents of Dogtown and Poverty Flats watched the river rise around their homes. Some tied their shacks to trees with steel cables. The water wagon man moved people to safety with his horse and wagon. The flooding clouded the water, contaminated wells, and dirtied laundry. High water threatened to wash out the swinging footbridge that workers and managers on the south side of the river used to cross to go to work. At the gas plant, floods threatened operations by clogging up the water intakes with logs, twigs, leaves, and other debris. During extremely high flows, the water reached the bottom of the plant bridge and breached the berm, flooding the lower terrace. None of the floods ever reached the buildings on higher terraces. Downstream, Black Diamond had its own troubles. Over the years the floods washed out the bridge and road, forcing its way into the lower part of the community.

Turner Valley Main Street, 1920s. (Glenbow Archives, NA-67-51)

The village responded with a dike. Sadly, at least one little girl and two little boys drowned during floods.

"Those little towns were really dumps" is how one oldtimer recalled the oilfield communities in the 1930s. And they were. More people lived outside the legal settlements than inside them. Ranchers found the invaders a nuisance. For those with a life-long commitment to a career on the land, the interlopers were latecomers with poor manners, dirty clothes, and insubstantial houses that spoke of impermanence. The fact that their cars invariably cost more than their homes said something to their agricultural neighbours.

The demand for instant housing created a market for the oilman's shack, built almost overnight by anyone with even minimal carpentry skills. Gerry Schultz was one of the thousands of men who flocked to the south end in the late 1930s. The rigs he visited had no work for unskilled labour, so he hired on to help Joe Leighton build shacks. Gerry and Joe became partners. They built a shack every two days. Gerry slept in the shacks they were building. A few weeks later Gene Denton of Anglo-Canadian came by and found him on top of a shack, installing shingles. Gerry didn't mind heights so Gene hired him to climb to the top of a 90-foot-high well, servicing rig and aligning pipe.

But before moving up in the oilfield, Gerry built dozens of shacks. The 12 x 24-foot model, with two rooms, sold for $235. The shacks sat on two six-inch square skids, not over eight feet apart, so a winch could pull them onto the back of a flatbed truck. Joists on two foot centres supported the floor. Wall studs and rafters were two feet apart. The roof was a quarter pitch, covered with 1 x 6 or 1 x 8-inch boards, tarpaper, and wooden shingles. They sometimes applied a "car roof" to save money: a lower roof, boards nailed across the roof, bent over a single lengthwise beam, rolled asphalt roofing applied quickly with a few roofing nails. Horizontal shiplap covered grey paper on the walls, which were in turn covered with black tar paper. (Carpenters applied the shiplap on the diagonal for their own homes—it was structurally stronger—but cut costs by putting it horizontally on the ones they sold to unsuspecting oilfield workers.) They sheathed the interior partition on one side and left the interior walls unfinished. The single inside doorway had no door. Other details included three windows and one outside door, all from the Cushing Mills in Calgary. The carpenters made about $20 a day, a fantastic wage at a time when unskilled labour came at a dollar a day. Dozens of men worked around the clock bashing together the crude shacks. Trucks brought lumber in 24 hours a day to the lumber yards that sprang up in each settlement. McFarland Lumber was the big timber supplier for the oil industry. Other companies included Eau Claire Lumber, Crown Lumber, and Royal Lumber.

One well-dressed man bought two of the shacks joined together with a small walkway. He operated a barber shop in one and a gambling joint in the other. He had previously operated a house of prostitution in Lethbridge, but only ran card games in the south end of the oilfield. RCMP Constable Smith would not tolerate blackjack so when the cop stuck his head in the barber shop, the gamblers in the next shed changed over to poker.

Most of the hastily built shacks served as homes. They rented for $5 to $15 per month. Some were very small, little more than a lean-to with two rooms. Families sometimes threw up a tent nearby for the children, in warmer months. Insulboard provided insulation in some homes. When a friend helped wire Geoff Andrews' house for electricity, he accidentally stepped on the Insulboard instead of the rafters and fell through the ceiling. Many shacks had cardboard boxes flattened on interior walls for insulation. Fruit boxes with curtains served as cupboards. A used furniture store usually sprang up in each settlement, selling junk or slightly better quality furnishings to the new residents.

Some families cut a trap door in the kitchen floor and dug out a small cellar for a storage area. Others dug a hole for a partial basement and pulled the shack over it. House lots were seldom larger than 25 x 50 feet, with an outhouse at back that served until the 1950s, or later. Most people rented a spot to perch their shack, usually from a farmer, or pulled the shack up to the rig site. When it came time to move, James and Reimer could do the job but if the big oilfield trucking company was busy, Johnny Schumacher winched up one end onto the back of his truck, lifted the other end with Simplex jacks and put a set of wheels underneath. He charged $4 per hour in the 1930s and 1940s. The move seldom took more than two hours. Johnny moved many shacks, houses, outhouses, churches, schools, halls, theatres, and other buildings. Movers often forded rivers when the bridges were too small for their loads. One lady stayed in her home during the move to keep an eye on her things. The truck got stuck while fording the river, leaving the woman unconcerned, rocking in her rocking chair while the workmen went for help. She later said she quite enjoyed the ride, especially the peaceful pause in the middle of the river. Another time Johnny moved a house from the south end of the oilfield to a beautiful view lot on the Elbow River in Calgary. As far as he could recall, it was the only building to cross the Glenmore Dam.

Snob Hill and Royalite Way

In direct contrast to the impermanent homes in much of the oilfield, Royalite's managers lived in the lap of luxury. The residents of Snob Hill with houses on each side of Royalite Way were of a different breed from the folk whose cars were bigger than their houses. Booms and busts came and went, and with them the small shacks, big cars and flamboyant attitudes of the Texans. But the gas plant managers who lived on Royalite Hill were more likely to ride out the cycles. The tree-lined main street flanked by 20 houses and surrounded by a golf course seemed permanent. The houses reflected the status of the residents as well as the company's commitment to southern Alberta's largest gasfield. While the average cost of other homes in the oilfield in the late 1930s was but a few hundred dollars, a fire commissioner's report listed the homes on Snob Hill as fully modern in the $5,000 to $6,000 range. Fire hydrants, a good supply of water, and a trained volunteer fire brigade provided protection against the fires so common in the rest of the valley. The inspector classified the area as a first-class insurance risk, well qualified to receive a special rate.

Oilfield Communities in the late 1930s

But Royalite's suburb of Turner Valley was the exception. Oilfield communities extended 17 miles from the northern limit at Millarville to the Highwood River in the south. Home Oil's camp just south of Millarville was a blaze of light, each house illuminated with gas lights. Closer to Turner Valley, houses at Whisky Row and Model Flats glowed in the harsh glare of the flares too. Lights at the North Turner Valley school cast their glow a mile north of the next village. Turner Valley and Black Diamond gleamed as in daylight as did their many squatters' settlements: Okalta Flats, Mortgage Heights, Poverty Flats, Dogtown, Cuffling Flats, and others. Further south lay Old Naphtha, Naptha, Glenmede, Boller

Royalite Oil Company party at Turner Valley Golf Course Clubhouse, 1940s. (Provincial Archives of Alberta, P2761)

Camp, Hartell, Mercury, Mill City, Little Gap, Little Chicago— later called Royalties after the discovery well, Little New York— later named Longview when the post office by that name moved to town, and finally, Little Philadelphia on banks of the Highwood River. From Sheep Creek in the north to the Highwood River in the south, the oilfield was a riot of flares, shacks, wells, and gas processing plants.

Although the Second World War boom was a welcome gift to the people in Black Diamond and Turner Valley, it came as a real shock to the farmers and ranchers in the south end. Teaching school in nearby High River, W.O. Mitchell recalled the feature that most impressed the locals, besides the nuisance caused by geophysical crews blasting off dynamite: "They caused dreadful hickups in the water supply. The other thing was the regular fart stink with the prevailing westerly winds, with great regularity. The euphemism for it now is sour gas. Well, I got news for them. It wasn't sour, it smelled just like a fart, or decaying, rotting, lockjaw steer, or whatever. The organic breakdown of stuff."

The *Calgary Albertan* could hardly believe the booming oil-towns at the south end of Turner Valley. On Saturday, June 25, 1937, a headline read: "You Don't Know Canada! Until You Have Seen the Flares, The Derricks, The Actual Piping of New-Found Flowing Gold, All In Alberta and Tourists From Everywhere Should Be Sure to Visit." In a full page of excited text and advertisements for oilfield businesses, the paper highlighted the amazing development of Little Chicago, which it speculated would soon be officially named "Prospect."

> Today a visitor to the new South Field in Turner Valley is confronted with a bristling forest of sky-reaching derricks spreading between the hills. Steel derricks, wooden derricks, piles of pipeline, mounds of muck, pools of dark muddy water with a trace of oil. Dotting this man and machine made panorama fiery flares from producing wells add to the unreality of the scene.
>
> The motorist drives right into the main street of Little Chicago. The road is flanked with restaurants, lumber yards, stores of every description; a dance hall, movie theatre, pool rooms, lodging houses, bachelor shacks, trailers and even tents. More than one hundred buildings, not all painted, have sprung up like mushrooms almost overnight, and every day adds another one. They are not ornate, nor architecturally perfect, but all are sufficient to meet the needs of many hundred oil field workers.

The visitor is sure to ask "What are all those fires?" for in every backyard in Little Chicago, Little New York and even in Hartell the ground spurts flame from small sunken spots. A close look reveals tin can dumps, for these holes house natural gas incinerators. There are no garbage collectors needed here, a network of pipes that snake the surface of the fields with little outlets everywhere takes care of refuse and waste, just the blackened tins remain.

The motoring tourist will have days of beautiful mountain views before reaching Calgary, but nowhere in the British Empire will his eyes behold a sight like "The Valley" with its flares, its derricks, its booming, relentless activity. The romantic story of discovery is unforgettably illustrated by that "Little Chicago" town. It's a trip all should plan to make and an experience none will live long enough to forget. You don't know Canada until you have witnessed the sight of Turner Valley's oilfield wonders.

Not to be outdone, The *Calgary Daily Herald* devoted almost the entire front page of its magazine section on Saturday, September 11, 1937, to "Turner Valley One of the Brightest Spots in Western Canada; Oil Community Residents are Good Earners, Good Spenders." The article reviewed current conditions in the booming south end, pointing out that the "depression which followed the 1929–30 boom taught many of these oil well workers a lesson they will never forget." Most had had no savings and went penniless into the tough times. Many learned to have a pleasant, if modest, life with less. Said one oil wife of the second boom: "Now it's different. We are earning good money again, but we know how to spend it to good advantage, and we know how to save—something we did not know in 1929."

Little New York (Longview) Main Street, May, 1938. (Provincial Archives of Alberta, P1932)

Store owners noticed different spending habits, especially in the more settled and sombre parts of the community. A clerk in a Turner Valley general store said: "People are undoubtedly more economical. In 1929, they would pay anything for special fancy groceries and think nothing of it. Today, most of them have their own gardens and are fixing up their homes as places in which to really live. We notice the difference in the sale of chintzes, cretonnes and so forth, which smarten up a home at small cost. In 1929, there was little pride shown in this respect. Home meant simply a place to hang your hat."

But the boom had gone to some heads. "The number of new automobiles in the oil communities is evident now. One young lady summed up the situation with the following observation: 'Why, in lots of yards, you will see a big car parked, and have to look twice to see the house behind it.'"

The *High River Times* reviewed the short history of the

south end of the oilfield in its Harvest and Oil Issue on October 6, 1938:

> You are greeted by a smell when you get a few miles from High River, but you're headed for the bright lights and the reason for the odour is very noticeable as the beacons of industry break into view. The lights of Turner Valley show up for hundreds of miles. Their history is young. The southern towns have mushroomed out of the prairies. The finest grazing land in this country has turned into roads, stores, and home sites; the stillness of the hills to the re-echoing thump, thump, thump of the drills. The places which carried the imprint of thousands of cattle hoofs, now carry the imprint of shoes made from their hides. The rush is on. Quick money still holds its lure.

Pioneers in Longview—Little New York—claimed all of two years residency at this point, led by Tom Kee who moved over from High River in 1936 to open the first store. Alf Baines and Neil Webster opened the first grocery store on March 1, 1937. Alf moved into the new community from the nearby Pekisko Store he operated with his mother, and Neil "cast his eyes out West from behind the bars of the Royal Bank" in High River. The partners built a 24 x 30-foot store from scratch and Alf used a tractor to pull a bunk car—for storage—and a cook car—to live in—in behind the shop. They rented the lot for $5 per month from a landowner, Mr. Twitchen, who charged $3 for residential lots. Alf locked the outhouse behind the store when too many muddy boots standing on the muddy seat put an end to goodwill. Then came the fateful night when, during a dance, two pretty women asked to use the facilities. Alf escorted them to the privy, unlocked it and returned to the party. Some time later Neil asked Alf "What happened to those ladies?" and Alf suddenly remembered sliding the lock through the hasp on the door, trapping the women inside the outhouse. The women never mentioned the incident but treated him with icy looks when they shopped at his store.

Gas came off a high-pressure pipe and provided heat for the buildings. Two fellows even connected a leaking pipe directly to their tent, oblivious to the consequences of running it under the storekeepers' bunk car. According to Alf, some men visited from Calgary and slept overnight in the bunk car. "They come in the next morning and they were just as white as ghosts. They sure looked sick, and they were sick. So I went out to see. The gas was leaking. The old floor, the shiplap floor, in the bunk car was dried up and was open, cracks in it, and this raw gas had come up through these cracks. It was just lucky there was six guys got out of there in the morning."

Running a store in the booming south end was more hard work than excitement. Alf and Neil tried keeping set hours of 7 A.M. till 10 P.M. but people banged on their door day and night. One woman dropped in for a pound of butter at 4 A.M. No one ever tried to rob the place and Neil just kept the cash in a little purse. They had no safe. Alf slept with the cash and a little .32 Ivor Johnson pistol under his pillow. The partners ran the store on credit with the grocery and dry goods suppliers, sending in orders with their travelling salesmen. Alf told the Scott Fruit man to make out the invoice to Webster and Baines and mail it to them at Little New York since the place at the top of the hill was called Little Chicago. When the letter finally arrived, it had seven tracing stamps on it. The invoice got to them after a circuitous route through New York City then to Calgary a second time, and finally to Longview.

Entertainment had its own flavour. Alf once went to the barber shop in Little Chicago where a high-stakes poker game sometimes broke out after minor players left the table. A fellow named George had rented a granary and set it up as a poker "establishment" only to have the RCMP officer from Okotoks walk into the granary. "George saw this policeman come in the door, so he took his eyeshade off, got up and went over to where he had a bunch of nails in the wall, to hang their clothes on. He went and got his coat and hat and put them on. The policeman says 'Where you going?' He says 'I guess I'm goin' with you, aren't I?' The policeman kind of laughed as he said 'You got any liquor in here?' He didn't, he wouldn't allow it. He says 'That's one thing I do not allow in that door, is booze, or anybody that's full of booze. There's no playing.' The policeman says 'You keep it that way' and walked out."

Another time, Alf, Neil, Homer Hayden, and another fellow drove an old car up the hill to sell 30 dozen eggs to storekeeper Rex Warman at Little Chicago. There was no road at the time, just tracks wandering up the hill. They ploughed through a mud hole where nattily dressed men struggled to free their trapped car. After delivering the eggs to Rex, they started down the grassy hill. Everything went fine until they hit an icy patch hidden under the grass. Down the hill they plummeted in a four-wheel skid. Homer Hayden jumped from the car without opening the door. At the last minute Alf saw an irrigation ditch but could not avoid it so Homer watched as his friends in the Model T bounced through the canal and down the hill. The car survived the incident without so much as a broken spring or a flat tire. "We used to have the odd lighter moments, alright."

Little New York, also called Longview. (Glenbow Archives, NA-3538-2)

Alf Baines sold out after just a few years. "I got fed up with it. It was a dirty, messy, stinky hole, I didn't like it. I just didn't like it."

The October 6, 1938, issue of the *High River Times* article gave the two southern oilfield towns a glowing report. Longview—Little New York—by the river had the Anglo Canadian Oil Company as its neighbour and client. In addition to 150 houses, the town boasted 600 souls, four general stores, storage companies, two drug stores, two theatres, the Twin Cities Hotel and its fine bar, a pool room, photographer, recreation hall, garages, barber shops, and a beautician. There were 12 restaurants and coffee shops with names like "The New York Coffee Pot—Home Cooking that Pleases" and "The Trocadero Café—A Good Place to Eat—Open All Night—Also Lending Library—Rate 2 Cents Per Day" and "Broadway Café—Home Cooked Meals in Home-Like Surroundings—Rooms and Board." There was even an outlet of the Riverside Iron Works of Calgary.

Little New York, born a month or two after its sturdy
twin Little Chicago, has made up for an early handicap
of age and is now a lusty on-comer. Although still less
than two years of age, it is true that Little New York's
building program has amounted to over $200,000 and
more to come. One of the happy features of these oil
towns is that there are signs of a second stage of development with attractive, substantial little homes in
evidence. Educational facilities are well cared for to
provide training for the growing number of little folk
in the towns. Little New York even boasts a law office,
where the knotty problems of life may be adjusted.

All this activity occurred in the midst of dozens of drilling
rigs working night and day to release oil from its prison far below
the surface.

Little New York's twin sat atop the hill. Little Chicago—officially Royalties—surrounded the 1936 discovery well with even
more activity. A thousand people inhabited 360 homes and shacks
and patronized stores including the Hudson's Bay Company and
Variety Furniture Exchange—"We Sell Only at Calgary Prices."
There were cafes with names like Spud Inn and Ma's Place, White
Owl Lunch, Flo's Jiffy Lunch—"Quick service–Good Eats," and
the Dinerette, as well as restaurants, a theatre, an ice rink, a drug
store, garages, storage yards, lumber yards with "Ready-Built
Cabins," and many other businesses as well as overfull schools
and a busing problem which sent the older students to the Turner
Valley high school. The oldtimers yearned for the good old days,
just a few months before. "The first few months the chaps were
up against real pioneering but the quick development and modern conveniences have made life soft and easy. They remember

the days when people flocked out to the district looking for work with no idea of what they were looking for or of what they were able to do. In those days every boiler house was full of tired and discouraged men when night rolled around. The old timers also complain about their poker games, and you can hear them wail that there are only about three players for every four games. Not like the old days, dad gummet! The old spirit is passing. The towns are losing their thrill and the people are getting too settled. Why even most of the boys have brought out their wives and you can't hold those house-warming parties, the charivarees, the birthday binges, and friendly get-to-gethers that used to be. Reckless money seems to be going and the conservative money is creeping in ...."

A Search in the Dark for a Future

In spite of the bustle of activity in the oilfield in the late 1930s, it was not a comfortable or convenient place to set up housekeeping. Amenities were hard to find and sometimes created an awkward transition for the family arriving in the oilfield on short notice. Freda McArthur's story shows how one immigrant became part of Turner Valley society in the late 1930s. Freda came from England to Millarville when she was eight. Her father had arrived in 1907, started a mixed farm and sent for the family two years later. On the crossing, the S.S. Lake Champlain struck an iceberg and sank, in the harbour in Newfoundland. When the older children got off the train in Montreal to buy a potty for the two-year-old boy, they nearly got left behind when the train departed for the West. A man in a large dog-skin coat greeted them in Calgary. He claimed to be their father and was there to take them to a grandiloquently named place, the Massingham Ranche, which turned out to be a small log cabin. For fun, the kids threw sheep heads into the river and then picked leeches off them and pretended to be physicians, administering the blood-suckers to their bodies. Freda remembered it as the best summer of her childhood.

As a young adult, Freda attended Central High School in Calgary. By 1919 she was teaching school near Consort, in east-central Alberta. There she met Walter James McArthur and she married the soldier in 1921. Walter's war service entitled him to a half section of land. They tried to farm but never got a single crop. The empty granary blew away along with the topsoil and their hopes.

Finally, their luck changed. One Friday in 1936 Walter got a call from his brothers, drillers in Turner Valley, saying "that if he wanted a job in the oilfield to be there by Monday." He called Freda home from her Women's Institute meeting—"Wild Indians" he called it—so they could pack. With their two little girls they prepared to leave Saturday midnight, after the locals "put on a dance and a do at the schoolhouse." The Model A car was in good shape. Into it they loaded their worldly possessions, the kids, a canary, and a few plants. Presents from the party included a set of silver engraved with their initials and a personalized quilt for the girls. "Be kind" said her husband's best friend as they left.

"We left in the middle of the night," Freda recalled years later. "It was in September, nice, beautiful weather. Something went wrong with the car. The lights weren't operating. I was wearing a pair of white shoes. I got out and walked ahead and Walt came slowly along behind, following my white shoes. That's all he could see."

Through the dark night they crept till they arrived at a friend's place. "We'd been invited to come for breakfast, so we came into their yard, me walking, Walt driving slowly behind with all this load of stuff. They gave us a good breakfast and then we came on to Calgary. He went out to the oilfields to start work and I stayed with Mother and Father in Calgary."

Walt worked hard but could not catch on to the work. Finally, he and other confused workers found out why. Ducky Welsh—he waddled when he walked—was left handed. He was teaching the new hands to wrap the chain, use the tongs and do everything else on the rig backwards, and they all found it difficult and very confusing. Walt worked his way through the ranks, eventually becoming a certified steam engineer.

Freda and the girls moved down to Hartell, into a series of shacks. They once dug up a potato patch for Mr. McKinnon in exchange for a sack of spuds. They rented a three room shack from a local at first. Into cramped quarters they moved their few possessions, a real bed and a Winnipeg couch, which folded down front and back for use as a bed. They had gas for light and heat. When the house across the road burned down, the locals pitched in some cash and helped build another shack. When they finally built their own house, Freda and eldest daughter Effie shingled it themselves.

The family only had running water when the kids trotted while carrying it home from the well. But rigs had hot water, so everyone went there for a shower. Two grown men once snared a gopher and threw it in the bath house "and the lady came running out, but she didn't have enough hands to cover herself."

Hartell families curled and they also skated at sloughs or ponds in the area. When Ralph Obourne fell, hitting his head on the ice, he said "It wasn't hitting my head on the ice that bothered me so much as the hollow sound." They played lots of card games, including crib and poker. The community put on plays and Freda wrote many interesting skits. The McArthurs loved fishing up the Highwood River and Walt was usually successful, though Freda took along a can of sardines, just in case. Walt and Freda celebrated their 25th wedding anniversary at the picnic shelter on the river, in the pouring rain.

Plentiful Gas for Light and Heat

The Turner Valley oilfield was famous for its flares, and it was the burning gas that made the oilfield glow on even the most overcast night. Flares at each well burned off the gas after primitive processing systems extracted the liquids. At each compressor plant, processing plant, and other oilfield facility, additional flares disposed of more gas. Pipelines snaked throughout the community, many on the surface, offering easy access to gas for anyone living near the line. Workers placed their shacks near

Tourists at oilwell, n.d. (Provincial Archives of Alberta, P1735)

their workplaces and took advantage of the cheap or free fuel. Each resident hooked up to the line in a time-honoured method. When Lawrence Barker's neighbour sent him to get a "two-inch saddle" from the hardware store, he wondered where they would find such a small horse. But Lawrence did as he was told. That evening, under cover of inactivity if not darkness, they clamped the saddle onto the pipeline that ran past his shack. Then, his neighbour hammered a punch into the pipeline through the mouth of the saddle. Up flew the punch, away flew the hammer and on went the valve cap to direct the gas flow through a pipe into Lawrence's new home.

Before gas conservation arrived in 1938, people paid $2 per month for an unlimited supply of gas, or just tapped into a nearby pipeline for free. Gas not only supplied heat in the shacks. Residents converted their wood-burning stoves to gas with a pipe through the side of the stove into the firebox with a cap on the end. Hacksaw blade cuts partway through the pipe let the gas escape, providing a primitive but effective burner. Gas lamp fixtures on the ceiling of each room burned more gas, and space heaters took the chill off the bedrooms. A little heater in the outhouse also took the chill off doing what came naturally in -40°F conditions. A small flare pit behind each shack served as an effective burning barrel for garbage of every sort. The more ingenious even devised another appliance: a flare in a pit covered with corrugated tin served as a block heater for the car.

Bill Lockhart recalled the story of a Calgary man who came to the valley looking for a home for his family. As a fireman for drilling rigs, he should have been more careful with gas. "He was getting the house ready to move his family out and there was a little knothole in the floor. He sniffed and smelled gas so he lit it. 'That's gas alright,' he said, 'it burns.' So he blew on it and that flame went down in that basement and it just lifted the building right off its foundations, knocked it fair far, but he wasn't hurt apparently. He admitted that he should have known better."

Although convenient, the gas was neither scrubbed of hydrogen sulphide nor safely controlled. The gas did not pose much danger when burned, though it made for an awful smell. Florence Denning claimed that anyone who burned it in their houses found all their house plants dead. Other anecdotal evidence suggests that the oilfield residents knew they were dealing with a toxic substance. Ralph Steen remembered that lead-based paint peeled off houses very quickly, especially those downwind from the gas plant and the diluted hydrogen sulphide gas that it dumped into the atmosphere. Bill Lockhart said that although he did not think sour gas bothered people, it certainly corroded the coating on barbed-wire fences. Nearby farmers and ranchers had to replace their fences often but Lawrence Watrin did not mind: as a driller in the oilfield he made enough money to pay off his mortgage on his ranch in 18 months, making almost $10 per day when farm labour made $25 per month.

Some people told stories of cooking a turkey in 20 minutes by merely turning up the heat so high in the cookstove that the steel glowed bright red. Gas pressure to today's furnaces seldom exceeds a few ounces per square inch, but gas pressure was not regulated in the oilfield. At times it pulsed through the lines at pressures up to 300 pounds per square inch while at other times it died out completely. Elmer Andersen recalled: "When we moved here, everybody had a flare in the burning barrel in the back alley, everybody had a flare in the outhouse to keep it warm so you didn't have to sit on that cold linoleum. That's when we come. That was called pioneering. There was no regulators on the gas and if you didn't watch, when you were lighting the stove, it would blow the lids right on the floor." Off the stove, that is, and onto the floor.

Pressure regulators, when available, could not handle large fluctuations. Besides, most houses did not have regulators. Fires burning in furnaces, heaters, and stoves flared up when the pressure jumped and went out when the gas flow stopped. Gas lines froze in winter and had to be thawed with steam. When the gas came back on, any ignition source could create a disaster. Bea Barker recalled that folks checked on each other after the gas went off and came back on, just to make sure everyone was safe. If the gas quit during the night, whole families could die when it began flowing again. Oilfield residents entered their homes with care, checking to make sure the furnace or heater was operating. Even still, lapses of common sense created catastrophic accidents. People sometimes lit a match to light the lamp before checking for gas. House explosions were not uncommon and deaths and bad burns happened too.

Insidious as it was, sour gas worked its way into every part of life, making the home nearly as dangerous as the workplace. After Melvina LaRosee married Frank Briggs, they rented a house from Mrs. Highland for $5 a month rent and got free, unscrubbed gas and a near disaster.

I got sick. My throat was sore and my eyes were running. I went over to my mother's and I said "I think there's a gas leak at the house." And the doctor had come in, he was called to a patient, and he said "Oh Melvina, don't be ridiculous, if there was a gas leak to such an extent that you'd have a sore throat and raw eyes, red eyes, you'd be dead. And think of the baby, the baby couldn't have lived through that." He said "There isn't a gas leak at your house." And I said "Well, I think there is." So we stayed at mother's for a day or two and I got a little better, so we went home. My throat was better and my eyes were better. The baby dropped something from her crib and I lit a match to pick it up, it was a dish that was on a little buffet thing there, and she stood up and knocked it down, and there were pieces there. So I bent over and lit a match. There was just one flooring, with spaces in between, nice and warm in the winter, I'm sure, and the flames just came up along in there. So I beat them out with a rug and when my husband came home I said "I'm glad tomorrow's your day off because you're going to fix that or I'm not going to stay here." So he crawled under the house. He had a very scientific way of finding out where the leak was, he lit a match. There was a little tub sitting over the cellar door, in the one room of the two-room shack, and the baby flew out of her crib, I dashed over and grabbed the baby in mid-air and the tub turned over and ran water all over the floor. Of course, my husband had immediately turned off all the gas when it did this and it froze there. My studio lounge was never the same colour again, all sooty. I thought the house was on fire but it happened that it just blew the wall and ceiling apart a little bit and there was building paper, and the sun was shining through the building paper and that was what I thought was the fire. It was quite an experience.

When times turned tough, the hazardous unscrubbed gas became a convenient excuse for house fires. Percy Wray sold house insurance during this period and recalled a rash of unexplained fires in shacks that belonged to the unemployed. Hopeless people with no cash could not even leave town, so an "accidental" fire in a shack in an oilfield that offered no employment provided a means of escape. With no market for the homes, many people burned them to the ground for the insurance money. As a result, insurance rates rose to 10 percent of the value of the property per year.

Sanitation and Health Care

Sanitation was primitive in the early days. Nearly every backyard had a fire pit or barrel with a gas flare burning day and night. Household garbage went into these infernos, solving a waste disposal problem. Outhouses took human waste but they were not a permanent solution in the booming settlements. Small lots and a large population quickly created the need for "honey buckets" in outhouses or inside homes. Lorraine Tourond recalled that these toilet pails in turn created a new job in the oilfield, and

Back alley in Little Chicago, also called Royalties. (Glenbow Archives, NA-2895-11)

men driving teams of horses pulled the "honey wagon" on regular rounds through the back alleys, collecting human waste for $2.00 per month.

Fresh water was a scarce commodity. At first, people found their own water, carrying pails from the nearest creek or well. Most oilfield people lived close to the oilwell that provided their income, and all drilling operations relied on large amounts of water, so many families got their water from the well. In the Turner Valley village, several waterwells strained to supply local demands. Finally, after spring runoff caused the outhouses in the village to overflow and contaminate the waterwells, local officials condemned all the wells and a spring southeast of the gas plant then became the only safe water supply. Various men including Carmen Alger, Dad Williams, Mr. Allan, Mr. Houghton, and Elijah Williams ran the water wagons and water trucks. In the south end, Mr. Graff and Johnny Schumacher delivered Highwood River water door-to-door from a 1,000-gallon tank mounted on a truck. Black Diamond water also failed to meet sanitation standards in 1930, and the town had to drill new wells. Spring floods often muddied the water supply from wells near the river. Charlie Woo treated muddy river water with alum which settled out the dirt. The gas plant eventually supplied water for the Turner Valley village, chlorinating it heavily during spring floods. Ethel Anderson said "It tasted awful, but it was wet." Her husband, Elmer, recalled that even the treated river water from the plant sometimes included the unexpected: one day he turned the tap on for a drink and a minnow swam into his cup.

Health care in the oilfield involved more than good drinking water. Until the late 1920s there were no health care professionals. Eric Mulder recalled that Sam Coultis' wife, Ruth, was a nurse and their house in Snob Hill was the first informal medical facility in the valley. As plant manager, Sam also had the only telephone. Tom Trotter recalled first aid men dealing with most medical problems when he began working at the plant in 1925. Their favourite treatment was tincture of iodine. Finally, in February 1928, Royalite hired Dr. A. Hall as company physician, and the boom in the late 1920s attracted more doctors to the oilfield. Royalite established a first aid station at Naphtha in 1929. Two doctors established practices in the valley that same year. Doctor Weissgerber opened a practice in an 18 x 32-foot building in Black Diamond, and Dr. Kenny worked out of an office in Turner Valley. One dentist visited Turner Valley and Black Diamond for a few hours each week, while another shared quarters with the Black Diamond doctor. The Black Diamond newspaper included an advertisement for a dentist in Okotoks. Private nurses also offered limited medical attention and served as midwives.

As a pharmacist, Joe Korczynski played an important role in the Turner Valley health care system. After three years as an apprentice in Vulcan, Alberta, he attended the University of Alberta in Edmonton for two years, graduating with the gold medal in 1929 for the highest marks in pharmacy. He then worked for the druggist in Okotoks, getting his introduction to the oilpatch through the various oilfield supply companies that served Turner Valley from the closest railway siding to the valley. In 1930 he bought the drugstore in Turner Valley just as the boom burst and his competition in Black Diamond went bankrupt. Joe's medical knowledge and prescription drugs helped the oilfield doctors minister to the community's needs. In tough times he even dispensed medicine to people he knew could never pay for it. On call round the clock, he became a central figure in the oilfield.

His pharmacy fitted the bill of an oldtime drugstore. He sold perfume, ladies handbags, men's wallets, chinaware, cameras, radios, and the many other necessities associated with a pharmacy. But his ice cream counter became the social centre for decades, serving five-cent pop and ice cream cones, candy bars, and anything else a sweet tooth might desire. The store almost closed during hard times, but when the oilpatch boomed, he hired two women to keep up with the business. He also trained apprentice druggists. Rationing during the Second World War forced him to limit chocolate bars and ice cream to the amount he sold the last year before the war.

Joe got to know almost everyone in the community. Remittance men from the United Kingdom had money to spend and no jobs, and so they passed time in the drugstore, telling stories about the old country. Whenever anyone new moved into town, locals sent them right down to Joe to take care of their headlights. The sulphur in the air quickly tarnished the silver reflectors in the car lights, turning them black, so Joe removed the covers and applied a coating of jewellers' lacquer to keep the reflectors from oxidizing.

When the second oilfield boom burst, all but one doctor moved away. Correspondence between Dr. Kenny and municipal affairs department officers responsible for the bankrupt villages shows that many patients were broke, too. The overworked doctor's own health deteriorated. Some months he gave away as much medicine as he received in salary. The village of Turner Valley paid him $50 once, but when an epidemic broke out in the valley in the fall of 1934, the call for Dr. Kenny brought him to the oilfield from his new residence in Calgary. Community health suffered so much in the mid-1930s that the Okotoks–High River Social Credit League passed a resolution in 1936 to appoint a medical officer for the oilfield to investigate epidemics and enforce quarantines.

With the renewed activity in the late 1930s, more medical professionals came to the field including Dr. Ardiel, Dr. Aziz, Dr. Blaney, Dr. Burke, Dr. Calahan, Dr. Victor Graham, Dr. Hall, Dr. Irons, Dr. Johnson, Dr. Key, Dr. Kinney, Dr. Pilcher, Dr. Soby, Dr. Smith, Dr. Townsend, Dr. Weisgerber and Dr. Wilson. Dr. Harry Lander and his cousin Dr. David Lander became legends, serving the oilfield people as emergency physicians in the field and from their offices in the Black Diamond Hotel. Itinerant dentists appeared in the oilfield again and visited south end communities one or two days each week. Finally, in 1943, the provincial government appointed Dr. Harry Lander as provincial medical health officer for the oilfield district and charged him with keeping the area safe and sanitary.

Doctors had their hands full in the oilfield. In one case, a family had to move away because the "residue in the air" was causing respiratory problems for the wife. Epidemics were also common. From 1930 to 1945 epidemics of smallpox, infantile paralysis, measles, sleeping sickness, mumps, jaundice, and scarlet fever swept through the district. Polio scared the oilfield community in 1938, affecting a dozen people by August. On September 1, 1938, Dr. David Lander diagnosed the 23rd case, according to the *Calgary Albertan*. "First symptoms were noticed Tuesday evening when the boy became slightly ill. Wednesday morning the boy was violently sick and Dr. Lander was summoned." District Health Officer Dr. A. Sommerville delayed the fall school season in the oilfield for two weeks for 28 teachers and 1,000 students. Of the 60 polio cases in southern Alberta that year, more than a third were in the oilfield, leading many to speculate that the public swimming pool by the gas plant was spreading the disease.

For a time, local ranchers and farmers avoided the oilfield towns, perhaps unjustly blaming the grubby villages and squatters' settlements for sickness. However, in many cases the disease spread because of unsanitary conditions or through contact between school children. Often, in order to control the spread of the epidemics, officials closed the schools and quarantined homes.

Less serious diseases also affected the community. On June 1, 1938, the Alberta government created a new level of provincial health care when it formed Okotoks–High River Health Unit. A first for Alberta, it was the direct result of the efforts of George Hoadley, the United Farmers of Alberta MLA for the riding until 1935. A review of health in the area showed that one quarter of the children suffered from malnutrition or had poor vision, and 50 to 75 percent had bad teeth. The study found 182 "defects" in the 300 oilfield children it examined. A provincial government agency eventually stepped in to counteract and prevent these medical problems with well-baby, prenatal, and life-extension courses which it held quarterly in Turner Valley and Black Diamond beginning in 1931, and again from 1937 to 1945. Baby clinics, dental clinics in the schools, Red Cross first-aid classes, home-nursing clinics, and mobile x-ray exams helped to prevent the everyday diseases common to the area.

Adequate hospital facilities arrived very late in the oilfield's development process. Doctors gave emergency treatment when possible, but serious cases went to Calgary, sometimes not surviving the long and bumpy journey. Drugstores in Turner Valley or Hartell provided some medication, but it was the late 1930s before a true hospital opened. Mrs. Rose LaRosee ran a small hospital throughout the 1930s, Alberta's first privately operated facility. She started it as a maternity facility, with two small shacks providing space for two patient rooms and five rooms for the LaRosees. Doctors Harry and David Lander encouraged Rose to expand the little facility for their male patients, so she added an operating room and a "bull pen," a room that could sleep four people at a time. At its largest, the hospital had five patient rooms. Rose charged $30 for a maternity confinement, including the delivery of the baby and a 10-day stay at the hospital, with meals. Her husband Nap—short for Napoleon—did the laundry out back. "Rose was a kind-hearted person," recalled her

Oil company office workers, 1946. (Provincial Archives of Alberta, P2685)

daughter, Melvina Briggs. A patient once paid with a large bath-
tub. Sometimes people could not pay their bills at all, but Rose's
response was that those unpaid invoices were stars in her crown
in the hereafter. According to another daughter, Viva Heyland:
"Mother passed away in April, 1960, and was put to rest beside
our father in the Okotoks cemetery. I'm sure that her star-stud-
ded crown is still shining."

Rose hired a nurse when things got busy. Many times, no
sooner did she hire a new nurse than one of the male patients
would marry her and Rose would have to look for another
caregiver. And so the little hospital earned a nickname: Rose's
Matrimonial Palace. When short of help, Rose pressed her daughters into service. One day she said "Melvina, run in and hold the
pan for the lady, she's going to be sick to her stomach." So the 12-
year-old did the best she could. Her older sister, Dolly, looked in
a few minutes later and found the patient throwing up into one
side of the pan and Melvina doing the same on the other. "Get
out of here," said Dolly, taking over. Recalled Melvina decades
later: "I wasn't much of a nurse, I'm afraid."

Local MLA George Hoadley unsuccessfully suggested that
companies withhold $2 per month from each employee to fi-
nance the construction of a suitable hospital. He also encouraged
the oil companies to build a hospital but said that an ambulance
was out of the question as the ride to Calgary took too long. The
editor of the local newspaper was supportive, too, writing that
"Oil field work being one of the most hazardous known, you
never know when you will need medical attention, and need it
badly, also in an immediate rush."

In spite of obvious demand for a hospital, the oilfield struggled through the 1930s with only company-sponsored first-aid
teams and the maternity hospital. The municipality refused to

build a new hospital, saying the province should pay for it with the windfall it was making from oilfield taxes and royalties. In 1939, locals proposed using the Legion Hall as a hospital, but a donated 40 x 60-foot former cookhouse opened in July as a 10-bed hospital. Local pioneer oilman Bill Herron Sr. donated the building and charged $30 per month rent on the land, including utilities. The small hospital was not self-sufficient and often had to ask businesses and the public for contributions. Locals eventually formed a hospitalization association with an office in Black Diamond. Monthly fees assured workers medical treatment in the facility. During 1943 and 1944, benefit dances were held to raise money to add rooms to the bulging hospital. Oil companies occasionally donated equipment to the cause. Mrs. Cora Burke and Miss MacLeod operated the hospital for years before handing over the expanded, 25-room facility to the municipality in 1948.

This hospital was always a special place, located as it was on the banks of Sheep Creek in a secluded spot at the west end of the Turner Valley village. Rick Smith was a frightened little boy when he had to spend time at the Turner Valley hospital, but he found a friend in the next bed. They made a ball out of paper and tape and played catch. Rick was sad to leave. Dr. David Lander once treated a Native boy at the hospital and encouraged his family to set up a tipi outside the boy's window so he would not feel alone.

Undertakers operated ambulance services in rural Alberta, and until the mid-1940s, the funeral homes in High River and Okotoks served the oilfield area. This disturbing conflict of interest finally ended in 1945 when the Alberta Petroleum Association offered to donate a used airforce ambulance to the cause. When no company, hospital, or municipality would accept the ambulance,

Percy Wray, Tommy Hayhurst, John Rice, John Houlden, and others formed the Turner Valley Ambulance Service. Percy thought it was probably the first ambulance service in Canada to provide free service to patients. The service charged half the going rate for ambulance work and billed insurance companies, the Workmans' Compensation Board, and various government agencies. The arrangement pleased everyone.

Percy worked on the ambulance for 25 years and four months. On his first run, he took a young child to Calgary. Accidentally shot with a .22 calibre rifle, the boy walked into the drugstore looking for help. Both Turner Valley doctors were out of town so Percy drove him to the city where x-rays showed the bullet had passed through the child's chest and down alongside his backbone without hitting a major organ. He lived.

Operating on a very tight budget, the Turner Valley Ambulance Service had no capital for a new vehicle. Things got so bad the men almost refused to drive the unsafe unit, which was falling apart and running on bald and frayed retreaded tires, only making a run if the patient was desperate. "A call came one Sunday morning from a rancher up the Highwood River," recalled Percy Wray. "We picked this fellow up and took him to the Turner Valley hospital. It turned out it was not a heart attack, but something quite similar." For part of the trip the worn-out transmission clashed and banged. Quite concerned, the rancher asked Percy, "Why don't you get a new one?" "That's easy, got no money." "Well," said the rancher, "go and take up a subscription." "No," replied Percy, "we've never gone begging yet." "Something's got to be done," continued the patient, "so take up a subscription and come and see me first." A week later the hospital called, asking Percy to visit the rancher in his hospital room. "You know, I've been laying in bed thinking about things.

I've got no family for my estate. I figure the government will get a bunch of money that they will spend unwisely—that I wouldn't appreciate. I've decided to spend a little bit myself. I've decided to buy an ambulance for you." And that's what he did. On Percy's advice, local legend and rancher Bert Sheppard chose a special vehicle for the job—a panel truck with high ground clearance for off-road travel. The rancher kept adding options to help it serve the public better, running up the cost. Bert also insisted on painting it red.

Life Without Universal Health Care

Workers and their families had many individual struggles in the days before government. A reliable ambulance system did little to counteract the absense of universal health care. One woman's story shows how a debilitating disease caused a family years of hardship. Bea Barker married Lawrence Barker on August 19, 1931, and moved to Turner Valley just in time to feel the full brunt of a major bust in the oilpatch cycle. The newlyweds rented a 16 x 18-foot one-room place in Cuffling Flats, on the south side of Sheep Creek. During an interview in their 60th year together, Lawrence quietly said to Bea, "Tell him about the years you nursed me." But first she talked about her children. Young son Syd once badly injured his arms trying to help his mother after the wind blew down a window. The local hospital was not due to open yet but Dr. Harry Lander put the young boy in overnight after removing shards of glass from his arms. The kids were quite rambunctious and often presented with open wounds so it got to be that "Dr. Harry Lander, whenever he saw Syd come, reached for a needle—that's the way it was." Tetanus shots were a common treatment against infection.

Her husband's problems started in 1941. "He was ill before that and we didn't realize it." Terrible pains racked his body on the job, walking line and field gauging, but he soldiered on. Intense pain sometimes paralyzed him. "They took x-rays and both of his kidneys were loaded with stones." Operation followed operation, seven in all. "Off and on, it went on this way for years." Medication didn't help. The last attack came in 1958. "It was a little rough on him, because he would go back to work and Dr. Lander would tell him, 'You can't go back to work' and he'd say, 'Well I have to, we have no hospitalization or anything.'" Bills piled up. They sold the car, cut back on other expenses, did without many things. The plant provided half pay of $43 every two weeks, and Bea stretched the finances as far as she could. "We'd sit down and work it out, see where we could give the hospital so much, the doctor so much." Hospital administrators were not always understanding. Once, as she brought her husband into the hospital in a wheelchair for yet another operation, the administrator called her into his office. "I went in and he said 'Mrs. Barker, you still have a hospital bill you haven't paid.'" She said "Look, do you want me to tell you exactly how much I get? I've got three children, I've got to come by bus, I have to feed and clothe these children and my husband is already on the way up to have another operation. Are you going to stop it?" "Oh no." said the administrator. So she promised, "When he gets back to work, and I don't know when because this time it's serious again and we don't know how things are going to turn out, I'll give you some money. Maybe it will only be two dollars a month." Bea had to pay the Turner Valley doctors, Calgary physicians in the Associated Clinic, bills for medicine. Things were tight.

The family took no holidays, bought nothing extra. Syd came home one day asking for more allowance. A kid at school got five dollars at a time—his Dad was a driller. Lawrence said to the boy "Well, son, we can't do that. We'll sit down and show you where the cheque goes." After supper they explained the family budget, the expenses and income, including a small allowance for each of the boys. Then Syd turned to his parents and said "Mother and Dad, you haven't got an allowance." The boys never mentioned it again. "So we never had any more trouble with allowances or anything and we said, 'Well, you'll have to run with the ones that don't get the five dollars every time they want it.'" Lawrence made toys, a big bobsled for the nearby hill, found skates.

Things finally turned around in 1958, and they built another home on the same lot. The newer place was much larger and they eventually installed electricity, indoor plumbing, and all the amenities of modern living. But they kept the outhouse, with a little gas heater. Their oilfield experience taught them that things are not always what they seem, that things can take a turn for the better, or the worse. So when the gas, water, or electricity went out in the 1990s, life continued.

Banking

Although not all fared well in the oilfield, business services arrived early to serve the commercial needs of the community. Some banking took place as early as 1919 at a small depot of the Union Bank of Canada in Black Diamond. When spring break-up made the roads impassable the next year, the manager of the Okotoks office chartered an airplane and personally accompanied the payroll to Black Diamond. The Royal Bank took over the Union Bank in 1925. At the intersection in downtown Turner Valley, the Royal Bank established its first Alberta "oil and gas branch" in 1927. The new branch attracted substantial deposits. Totals in current and savings accounts during the development period were: 1930: $971,000; 1935: $719,000; 1940: $1,113,000; 1945: $2,109,000. Although the branch suffered economically during 1932 to 1934, throughout the development period it consistently equalled, or, as in the case of the years 1940 and 1945, generally exceeded the deposits on hand at both Royal Bank branches in Okotoks and High River. The Canadian Imperial Bank of Commerce also opened a branch during the boom of the late 1920s and operated it from October 9, 1929, until March 21, 1934.

Telephones

There were a few telephones in the oilfield before 1924, just country line extensions on the Okotoks telephone exchange. In 1925 the Highland Oil Company began lobbying local MLA George Hoadley for better oilfield telephone service. In its letter to the politician, it claimed that "eight or ten" other wells "in close proximity to the Highland well" also needed a better link with the outside world and the anxious shareholders who were always calling for information on their investments. New lines became available in late 1926.

Several Black Diamond companies subscribed immediately to the new telephone system including Canada Southern Oil Company, the Illinois-Alberta Oil & Refining Company, and the Herron Cartage Company. Both Home Oil and Imperial Oil had oilfield offices and telephones in Okotoks. The Turner Valley outlet of the Royal Lumber Yard took a telephone in 1926. By the end of 1928 there were telephones at the machine shop, the cafe, and the lumber yard in Turner Valley. A trucking firm took

Turner Valley telephone switchboard, n.d. (Provincial Archives of Alberta, P3069)

a phone in 1929 along with a bakery, the maternity hospital, a branch of the stock-brokerage firm of Solloway Mills, a drug store, a grocery, and a men's wear store. Burns and Company Limited listed a phone at its meat market by the beginning of 1931. The Alberta Provincial Police appeared in the directory that same year along with various service and supply companies. A few private citizens also subscribed to the telephone system.

By the 1950s a telephone was a common part of nearly every home, but the telephone switchboard was still a totally manual system. Florence Denning recalled working the switchboard from 1952 to 1955. Mostly it was boring work. She worked nights at first, sleeping on a cot. The night shift lasted from 10 P.M. to 8 A.M. Oil company men rang each other during the night and woke her up to make the connection. Operators were not allowed to listen in on the conversations on the telephone, but they had moments of excitement even still. During lightning storms, sparks of electricity jumped out of the plug-in holes in the switchboard, right beside her as she was working. The lightning strikes always frightened her, but she needed the job.

Schools and Churches

By 1928 oilfield residents were straining the public school system. The local schools amalgamated in 1929 and the greater tax base allowed for more schools in the two communities. A Calgary contractor added four new rooms to the Turner Valley school in 1930. The school district built a new school four miles southeast of Hartell to serve that part of the oilfield, but disgruntled Hartell residents complained in the local newspaper. With the influx of oilfield workers, the new school was far from their settlement, and they felt powerless, outnumbered as they were by Black Diamond and Turner Valley residents. New construction did not solve crowded classroom conditions. Some children attended classes in churches and other makeshift classrooms in Black Diamond and Turner Valley. At the school at the north end of Turner Valley, the noise from Hell's Half Acre made it hard for Jean Harris to concentrate on her schoolwork. Crowded conditions in schools continued until the end of the Second World War.

Churches were popular in the oilfield from the earliest days. The Catholics attended mass in homes and in local schools beginning in the early 1920s. By 1930 the United Church, Church of Christ, Undenominational, Catholic, Pentecostal, and Anglican congregations all had buildings in the valley. These churches sponsored choirs, women's organizations and children's clubs, and catered banquets to raise funds for their favourite charities.

Rationing During the Second World War

The third boom was great—until war broke out. On the home front, strict rationing meant limits to nearly everything: sugar, meat, dairy products, candy bars and ice cream, liquor—the list was long. One day one of Melvina Briggs' daughters came dancing into the house with a handful of sugar coupons that she found, thrilled by the thought of a birthday cake dripping with icing. Florence Denning grew accustomed to using much less sugar in canning during the war and found prewar products excessively sweet. She remembered when they replaced peanut butter with soy heart, a horrible substitute.

Rationing affected other parts of life too. Cement and most building materials were hard to buy, and people dusted off scavenging skills from the Depression to make do during the war. Service stations closed on Sundays and rationing coupons severely limited sales of car tires and gasoline to civilians, so many people parked their cars and walked to work. Maurice Edwards adapted another strategy, driving his car through town, picking up men on his way to work and using their ration cards for gas and tires. Strangely enough, the war accelerated the transition from animals to tractors on the local farms. Alex Hartell recalled that the shortage of seasonal labour forced many farmers to adapt mechanical implements to do the work previously done by hired men.

Women's Groups and Activities

Women's groups were numerous. At Hartell, the women formed a bridge club in 1930. In Black Diamond and Turner Valley the United Church women organized ladies' aid meetings and teas that year, and Turner Valley women formed a branch of the

Women's Institute on November 1, 1930. During its decades of continuous service the Institute raised money through raffles and banquet catering. The proceeds went to support cancer research, general health research, cemetery upkeep, and the construction and maintenance of a swimming pool.

The Turner Valley pool was famous throughout southern Alberta as one of the only public outdoor pools that operated year round. Mrs. Brown of the Women's Institute, while on a walk with some other women, saw hot water coming out of Royalite's steam plant and going to waste in the river. She decided it could be used in a swimming pool. They got volunteer labour to dig the pool and started running it as part of their service to the community. Mrs. Calderwood, who lived in a house on the north side of the pool, operated it for many years. According to Ethel Andersen, "The pool operated smoothly until the sulphur plant came into being and the health authorities felt it was a hazard to health and they were asked to install filters. We couldn't afford to install them. I always told them they had a sulphur bath and a mud bath at the same time, and they enjoyed it." The Women's Institute eventually closed the pool at the end of the summer of 1960 when the health department demanded they install filters.

Not all women participated in these social activities and some experienced loneliness. Women were stuck at home with rationing and young children while their men went off to excitement and adventure at war. Pat de Mille found the wartime years rather dull. She sometimes took the morning bus to Calgary to buy children's clothing, returning in the afternoon—her big entertainment. Unfortunately, many pictured in the Roll of Honour pages in the local history book have an asterisk beside their names, an indication that they did not return alive.

Children's Activities

Besides taking swimming lessons at the pool, oilfield children seldom were at a loss for things to do. They had school work, music lessons, and chores. When not playing in the bush or in the creeks—they could only stay in the creek that ran through Hell's Half Acre for a few minutes, the water was so hot—or hiking west into the hills, they attended formal clubs. The Black Diamond United Church provided a "Tuxis" discussion and social club for teenage boys beginning in 1930. Some oilfield children took music lessons and won prizes in a music festival in Calgary in 1933. The activities of Boy Scouts and Girl Guides groups also entertained oilfield children.

Adult Entertainment

With rough roads to negotiate to the worksite, there wasn't much leisure time between the 12-hour shifts that were common in the early days. Even still, many men found time to tip a bottle and play poker. The first legal bar opened in Black Diamond in 1929. It did not take long for the women of ill repute to show up either, usually following the banker out from Okotoks on payday. As things became more settled and the community grew, Royalite donated an old bunkhouse as a community hall. It had a small reading room at one end and the main part hosted many dances. Some workers took up the banjo, trumpet, accordion and violin, while others played the drums and piano. Before long the community boasted a fine little dance orchestra. Weekend dances became common. While the music played indoors, bottles of bootleg, contraband, and legal spirits came out of compartments in the cars outside to add to the festivities. The police attended the dances and knew the bootleggers well. One was handicapped, in a wheelchair and made his living selling alcohol and running a gambling operation.

Dances at the end of the 1920s pointed to a new trend in the social life of the oilfield: a more stable community. As the field matured and men saw the possibility of a career, they moved their families to Turner Valley. But they first had to find a home. There were none for sale, so men like Bill Lockhart built their own and helped others. "No one was rolling in dough, so the usual things was to pick a spot and get the lumber there, have a couple of cases of beer on hand and as we did not then work on Sunday, a group of us would put the framework up and get the roof on over the weekend. What if we did sometimes cut the rafters with a crosscut saw, everyone was in a happy frame of mine and we did get the job done. Joe Jackson [a native son of Millarville] and I had worked together doing carpenter work for the company when things were slack so the people looked to us to find time through the week to put in the doors and windows. We did not do this for money. In those days you did not charge your friends when you were in a position to help them with something and both of us like that kind of work." Each house had an outhouse nearby.

Men expanded their entertainment once their families arrived. They formed an official club called the "Oil Worker's Society" but changed its name to the "Driller's Inspirational Angora Society." Highly irreverent papers and musical numbers provided entertainment: one tenor sang a solo called "Oh, for a Single Hour of Bliss" but modified the words to "Oh, for This Hour of Single Bliss." Black Diamond men organized an Elk's lodge, formed a radio club, and opened a branch of the Canadian

Legion in 1931. Entertainment for men and women depended on their economic status. Most of the hundreds of unemployed or poorer residents could not afford the bus trip to Calgary for a movie or a dance, or even automobile transportation to the local theatre, dance, or party at the other end of the oilfield.

Curling, Softball, Polo, Golf, Hockey, Fishing

Sports varied from individual activities to semi-professional pursuits. Oilmen began curling in 1926. Two-minute boxing bouts entertained men at a Legion smoker in Turner Valley in 1930. In the early days, there were numerous softball teams. Only

Alberta's first Oilers hockey team. (Glenbow Archives, NA-67-46)

the catcher had a mitt. Teams with uniforms competed at the baseball diamond at Sport's Day on July 1. During 1931 men formed a Polo and Hunt Club and a Fish and Game Club. The Turner Valley high school rugby team suffered a miserable 13 to 5 defeat to the High River squad later that year.

Sam Coultis' lone house on the hill south of the river found itself surrounded by more homes as the plant grew. The hilltop community housed Royalite managers only, providing company houses on both sides of a street called Royalite Way. Nonresidents called it Society Heights, Nob Hill, or even Snob Hill. Its name fit even better when the company developed a golf course around the homes and by 1930 it boasted a Golf and Country Club. The Royalite Golf and Country Club was a member of the Alberta Golf Association and had nearly 50 members, each paying a $50.00 membership fee. Sam Coultis was the first president of the Golf and Country Club in the early years. The members laid on "delicious meals" for themselves on the golf course grounds.

Royalite also boasted a semi-professional hockey team and the oilfield sponsored it with pride through both booms. The first team, called the Imperials, played in the Southern Alberta Senior Amateur Hockey League from 1929 through 1931. The Turner Valley Oilers (and no, they did not move to Edmonton decades later!) represented the oilfield from 1938 through 1941 when companies again imported and employed hockey players from around western Canada.

Serious loners could fish day or night in the oilfield. Plant manager Tom Trotter remembered fishing at night by the light of the flare just upstream of the gas plant on Sheep Creek. Ducks and geese frequented the spot too. Black Diamond storekeeper Charlie Woo recalled another reason for catching fish upstream of the plant: he claimed oil leaks into Sheep Creek contaminated the fish in the 1960s, and he did not like the taste of fish flesh that smelled of sulphur. He ate it a few times, but it did not make him feel good. Men also went hunting in the mountains.

Politics

For those who took their extracurricular activities seriously, politics was always a controversial topic in the oilfield. The prairie provinces did not receive control over their natural resources when Ottawa created them, but Alberta started lobbying for rights almost from the start. For 25 years the province struggled with the federal government and finally, in 1930, it received the right to the benefits from the resources as well as the responsibility to regulate and control their use. It turned out to be a much larger job than anyone imagined. Since early Alberta operators

Royalite Christmas Party, Dec. 20, 1951 at the Palliser Hotel. (Provincial Archives of Alberta, P3033)

had to report to the Department of the Interior, they did not
have free reign like their counterparts in Texas and Oklahoma.
But when producers began flaring gas in Turner Valley in order
to produce liquids, Ottawa's attempts to control the waste failed.
Alberta watched much of the potential profits from the oilfield
go up in smoke and vowed to restrict the process once it gained
control. It established the Turner Valley Gas Conservation
Board in 1932, but producers appealed to the courts to prevent the province's attempts to control the waste. In 1938, the
province finally created the Alberta Petroleum and Natural Gas
Conservation Board and began shutting in waste gas, forcing
producers to find markets or keep the resource in the ground.

      Government regulation affected life in the oilfield in vari-
ous ways. At first, the booms excited imaginations, and visions
of great wealth and power danced in the heads of oil promoters, speculators, politicians, and many others. The reality was
less spectacular. The 1914 boom lasted only a few months. The
1924 boom lasted until the early 1930s, generating more hope
for long-term benefits, but largely failed to fulfil the grandiose
dreams. Instead of seeing the windfall profits as a large pie to split
among many players, each oilpatch group expected the wealth
to fall only to them. As a result, fights broke out over the spoils.
Turner Valley was no different. Landowners complained about
the roads the oilmen ruined and demanded that oil companies
repair the potholed trails. Industry representatives pointed to
their high taxes paid and said governments should fix the roads.
Politicians said the oilfield roads were the best in the province
and suggested that landowners and oilmen work out a private
agreement if they wanted a better transportation system. In spite
of complaints, politicians tended to treat the oilfield well. As a
source of considerable provincial revenue, the Okotoks–High

River riding received special attention from the United Farmers of Alberta government.

For the constituents, it was never enough, of course. In the early 1930s, the Social Credit party held bean suppers in Turner Valley to attract supporters. George de Mille attended, perhaps only partly because his father was a Conservative. As old age and corruption had settled into the tired old UFA political party, locals learned that the only gravelled road in the constituency was from Macleod Trail to their MLA's home. People were ready for a change and Social Credit offered a new vision for government. School teacher and part-time minister William Aberhart spoke persuasively, mixing religion and politics into a seamless philosophy that attracted the disenchanted poor to the new party in 1935. In Turner Valley, Social Credit meetings packed locations including the Log Cabin, the school, and theatres.

It was no accident that oilfield residents showed so much interest in the Social Credit party and its candidate, William Morrison. People in the booming oilpatch expected special treatment and when Alberta gained control over its natural resources in 1930, oilfield residents sent a petition to the legislature:

> Resolved that we the workers in the Oil Fields, generally known as Turner Valley, urge upon the Special Committee of the Legislature dealing with Redistribution in the province that consideration be given to the creation of an electoral district in our territory in order that this growing industry may have the opportunity of electing a member to represent the oil industry in this section of Alberta. The ever-increasing population in this district warrants such provision being made.

The province did not create a special riding for the oilfield so when Social Credit groups sprang up before the 1935 election, many people joined the new party, expectantly awaiting a new government. On voting day the Social Credit candidate took an impressive two out of three votes from the incumbent, but oil-field polling stations gave five times as many votes to the Social Credit candidate.

William Aberhart was a busy man before the election, teaching school and preparing weekly live radio programs in addition to running a new political party. Unsure of his party's elector-al success, he refused to run in the election and risk becoming an opposition member. When his party won the election and formed the government, he needed a seat. William Morrison graciously stepped aside in the Okotoks–High River riding and Aberhart won the seat in an uncontested by-election. Although it later won an award for standing up to Social Credit attempts to muzzle the Alberta press, the *High River Times* gave its enthusiastic support to the premier representing the Okotoks–High River constituency in 1935.

Unfortunately, hopes that the premier would give the riding exceptional representation in the legislature quickly faded. Constituents petitioned for a health officer and the licensing of labour. They called on the premier to enforce hours-of-work legislation to create more jobs, to restrict imported labour, and to repair the horrible oilfield roads. When a Social Credit group wrote repeatedly, begging the premier to investigate the frequent epidemics, Aberhart's reply showed his irritation. Although he had only been in power for a year, he had appointed a High River doctor to investigate and he wrote saying, "if he is not attending to his duty, surely I should not be blamed for that."

Social Credit philosophy included a deep distrust for na-

Highwood River at Guy Weadick's ranch west of High River, n.d. (Provincial Archives of Alberta, P6594)

tional financial institutions, corporations it suspected were controlled by an international Jewish conspiracy. Alberta's radical Credit House Act and the Social Credit Measures Act in 1936 threatened to control the banks and cancel interest payments incurred before 1932. The banks were not amused. In Turner Valley, this distrust caused problems for oilfield residents after the 1936 boom. A Dominion government program for permanent housing failed because of Alberta's political climate. In the *High River Times* in 1938, a mortgage lender who was making funds available for construction in other provinces stated he could not risk his money in the radical province—he refused to lend money to people in the High River area or the oilfield.

Aberhart's version of Social Credit ideology also promised a monthly $25 dividend to each Albertan because, as he saw it, banks were to blame for the "poverty in the midst of plenty" that flourished in the 1930s. By printing and distributing "social dividends" he expected to jump-start the provincial economy and seize control of the financial system from the international financiers and return it to "the people" through his party. The logic appealed to many Albertans and, although it threatened banks, it did not threaten capitalism. Besides, westerners easily accepted conspiracy theories that blamed the CPR, Ottawa, and the large banks for the Depression. Unscrupulous capitalists were easy targets, and Social Credit propaganda promised to solve Alberta's financial woes.

Within days of winning the election, Aberhart started backing off on the more radical aspects of the Social Credit platform. The day after the election, hundreds of people lined up for their $25 monthly "social dividend." It did not come. A week later Aberhart said that 75 percent of his voters did not really expect the $25, just a reordered society that would allow them to get back to work. Seeds of protest grew. When the money came—specially printed Social Credit scrip, not cash—merchants accepted it grudgingly. Turner Valley druggist Joe Korczynski said the Social Credit "funny money" was a burden on shopkeepers, and he was careful to return it as change to Social Credit supporters.

Most oilfield residents supported Social Credit in the mid-1930s but those that did not sometimes found it hard to make a living. Percy Wray lost his job as secretary-treasurer for the two bankrupt communities, Black Diamond and Turner Valley—because he opposed Social Credit. When the government asked him to submit a letter of resignation, he did. Local ratepayers rallied around him and encouraged him to stand up for his job. The deputy minister investigated and found that four of the five Social Credit men who signed the letter asking that Percy be terminated were not ratepayers. In fact, they were on relief. Percy withdrew his resignation letter and heard nothing more of the incident. His paycheque continued.

Then the forest ranger west of Turner Valley was fired while snowbound one winter far west of town. He also opposed Social Credit. Locals nominated Percy to go to Calgary and "beard the lion in his den" by talking to Aberhart about the dismissal. Percy asked the premier to investigate the firing of Freddie Nash, and Aberhart replied, "Well, my son, no one need fear for his job who does his work properly. You can tell Mr. Nash that he has nothing to fear for his job until we look into the matter." He too held onto his job.

By 1936 local discontent with the premier and the Social Credit party was brewing to a boil. Jim McInnis, for a time the mayor of Turner Valley, recalled a story about politics: "No rats in Alberta?" a worker at the plant once said, referring to the province's policy of keeping the rodents out in order to protect the grain stores, "That place up in Edmonton is full of rats." As far as he could remember, everyone at the plant opposed Social Credit.

Irene Dyck arrived in Turner Valley in 1931 as a school teacher. A lifelong socialist and major financial supporter of the Alberta New Democratic party, she considered Aberhart "a drip." She remembered hearing cackling chickens on his live radio shows. When Aberhart came to the riding, her husband Jack Dyck and others ran him out of a meeting, badgering him so much he escaped through the back door. Jack later borrowed a horse and went door to door through the constituency, collecting signatures on a recall notice. They also collected $200 to go with the petition. Social Credit policy allowed constituents to recall their elected member by signing a petition and asking for a by-election.

People from all walks of life signed the petition recalling Premier Aberhart. The unemployed wanted a change in the hours of work, from 12 to 8 hours per day, to make more jobs. They also attacked the Social Credit government for chasing capital from the oilfield with radical banking ideas. The local newspaper accused the premier of eliminating jobs with his proposed conservation legislation. Oilfield work slowed in the politically uncertain climate. The drilling companies, often out of work themselves, had full work crews and as many as 20 or 30 men on waiting lists to join their operations if and when work became available.

The recall petition even included members of the local Social Credit study group. Since the government was making enormous profits from the oil and gas industry, they thought the premier's attitude to the Okotoks–High River riding amounted to neglect. They wanted a more responsive member in the legislature. The premier responded: "I think I know from what source the trouble is arising in my constituency …." Indeed, letters to the premier from September to November, 1937, had listed "financiers," intimidation by oil company officials, and the poor conditions of the oilfield roads among the petitioners' reasons for the recall. While intimidation practices perhaps encouraged some people to sign the recall petition, the Social Credit was clearly losing support in the riding. By 1939, all the members of the Turner Valley Social Credit group had let their memberships expire. No one in Royalties renewed, and in Black Diamond only one-third of the previous supporters remained faithful until 1939.

Although the Social Credit government repealed the recall act in the fall of 1937, Aberhart left the riding as quickly as he arrived, allowing another Social Credit candidate to campaign in the 1940 election. In Black Diamond, Hartell, Lineham, and

Longview, the independent candidate narrowly defeated the Social Creditor, while in Turner Valley and Royalties the Social Credit candidate won by a small margin. In the riding as a whole, however, the Independent candidate took four votes to every three received by the Social Credit candidate. By 1944, the next provincial election, the oilfield was once again prospering under wartime conditions. A Social Credit member returned to the legislature with a substantial majority in each oilfield polling station, if only by just a slight majority in the whole riding.

Chapter 6

The Story Continues

D ay and night the trucks rolled through Alberta's first oilfield, moving rigs, equipment and supplies north to Leduc. The February 13, 1947, discovery of oil near Edmonton eclipsed the Turner Valley oilfield almost overnight. Landmark events have a way of making everything else fade, for a time. Ontario's Petrolia oilfield boomed in the 1860s, Turner Valley caught the imagination in 1914 and again in 1924 and 1936, Leduc flared up in 1947, Pincher Creek and Redwater in 1948, Golden Spike in 1949, and the list went on into the 1950s, 1960s, and 1970s. In the 1990s, new development off the East Coast promised another boom. Continental pipelines linked Alberta's abundant oil and gas wells to markets in central Canada and the United States to British Columbia, Washington, Oregon, and California on the West Coast. One massive development scheme after another took attention away from Turner Valley. Most frightening of all, Alberta's first oilfield residents watched as friends and neighbours moved away, their homes disappearing down the road on the back of big trucks. Royalties disappeared in a few years, Hartell, Naphtha, Boller Camp, Mill City, Sterling Road, Glenmede, and many other settlements dried up and blew away.

But oil remained in the rock, and gas too. Although flares consumed billions of cubic feet of gas in the days before the

THE OIL AND GAS JOURNAL

"Oh me! Here we go—automobiles, colleges, taxes!"

(Provincial Archives of Alberta, P1827)

conservation board reined in unscrupulous production, gas production continues. The Dominion Oil Controller opened the
taps on Turner Valley's oilwells during the Second World War, and
they produced nearly 10 million barrels of oil each year, an unprecedented amount for Canada. Even still, oil production only
barely dented the oilfield's reservoir. Many hundreds of millions
of barrels of oil are still trapped in the ground below Turner Valley.
Even the severely depleted stores of natural gas still hold many
decade's supply for southern Alberta consumers. But glory and
excitement in new oilfields stole the spotlight from Turner Valley
as they took the exploration, drilling, and construction people.

Moving trucks did not drag every shack and small house
from the unincorporated oilfield settlements. They deposited
some buildings in Black Diamond and Turner Valley, bolstering
these villages. Census figures show 683 people living in Black
Diamond in 1931. It grew to 890 residents in 1941 and 1,380
in 1945, fell to 1,154 in 1951 and 991 in 1956 and recovered to
1043 in 1961, then dropped to 858 in 1966 and recovered again
to 945 in 1971, dropped to 1,444 in 1981 and then grew to
1,486 in 1986 and 1,623 in 1991. Turner Valley showed a similar pattern, growing from 656 in 1931 to 676 in 1941, 1,157 in
1945, 719 in 1951, 704 in 1956 and 702 in 1961, 625 in 1966,
766 in 1971, 1,311 in 1981, 1,271 in 1986, and 1,352 in 1991.
The Municipal District of Foothills No. 31 which included both
Black Diamond and Turner Valley had a total of 13,887 residents
in 1991. In the 1991 census, the 25–44 age bracket shows the
largest percentage of the population for these towns. Although
many oldtimers retired in the area, the high percentage of younger people proves that the towns will grow. Unfortunately, many
of the working-age people commute to Calgary for a job, and
local employment in the oilpatch is scarce. Buses take oilfield

residents to Calgary to work, whereas in the boom years the buses took them to the city for shopping trips and appointments.

By contrast, the south end exploded in the late 1930s and early 1940s, peaked during the war, and then almost disappeared as drillers moved to Leduc and Redwater. The townships that contained Longview, Royalties, Naptha, Hartell, and several other unincorporated settlements grew from a population of just over a hundred souls in 1921 to 777 people in 1931, to 1,019 in 1936 and then almost tripled to 2,996 in 1941 before dropping off to 1,881 in 1945, 1,247 in 1951, 362 in 1966, and 357 in 1971. Although the census did not publish population for these townships in 1956 and 1961, it listed unincorporated settlements of 50 people or more. Royalties appeared with a population of 278 in 1956, 156 in 1961 and just 14 in 1991. By 1991, the census listed 13 people at Hartell and 27 at Naphtha. Millarville boasted just 43 residents in 1991. The oilfield boom certainly stands out as the high point in the history of these communities.

Is the story over? Does the old oilfield's forgotten status mean its days are over? Definitely not. Nowhere else in the Canadian West can we find an abandoned gas plant that dates to the early days of the western Canadian petroleum industry. The Turner Valley story is the basis for understanding the role of oil and gas in western Canadian society. Natural gas heats our homes and gasoline products fuel our cars and create thousands of jobs for Canadians. New developments in oil sands, northern oilfields, and offshore development only prove the significance of the oil industry to the Canadian economy.

The Turner Valley story began on a surface seepage. Canadians invested in the dream of an oilpatch and the 1914 discovery well rewarded their hopes. As Turner Valley grew into

the largest oilfield in the British Commonwealth, it attracted
the attention of international economic forces. By the 1920s,
Alberta's first major oil and gas reserves were firmly in the control
of Imperial Oil, a subsidiary of the American company, Standard
Oil of New Jersey. Independents struggled to retain partial control over this oilfield, but developments in the late 1930s created
an even stronger link between Turner Valley and larger forces.
When the Second World War broke out, the oilfield became
part of a continental military strategy that even involved training airplane pilots for British Commonwealth defence. Pipelines
eventually linked Turner Valley oil and gas into the continental
pipeline grid and made it another part of a commodity system by
the end of the century.

Bar at Turner Valley Golf Course Clubhouse, 1940s. (Provincial Archives of Alberta, P2772)

All these events affected the lives of the people who lived and worked in this oilfield. Once Turner Valley attracted international attention, Canadians had to compete with Americans for jobs in this field. Gas processing and oil collection systems fed Turner Valley production into the southern Alberta economy. These systems operated under unique Canadian laws, and Alberta politicians also added their flavour to the development process. The oilfield's proximity to Calgary also affected its evolution. Many factors created a unique economic and social situation in Turner Valley. As a result, residents of western Canada's first major oilfield experienced life in unique ways. Their lives tell the story of oil and gas in the Canadian West.

More Great Alberta Books

Cattle Kingdom: Early Ranching in Alberta
by Edward Brado

"A book that deserves a place in the library of anyone interested in Western history." *Lethbridge Herald*   *$19.95 paperback. ISBN 1-894384-57-1*

The Game of Our Lives
by Peter Gzowski

This best-selling hockey classic tells the incredible story of the Edmonton Oilers' 1980-81 season when the team was poised on the edge of greatness. *$19.95 paperback. ISBN 1-894384-59-8*

Denny's Trek: A Mountie's Memoir of the March West
by Cecil Denny

In this frontier epic, Denny tells the amazing story of how the Mounties originally came west in 1874 to deal with the renegade whiskey traders, and to set the stage for peaceful settlement.
$17.95 paperback. ISBN 1-894384-43-1

Suburban Modern: Postwar Dreams in Calgary
by Robert M. Stamp

A fascinating examination of how the suburbs rather than the downtown defined Calgary's particular approach to modernism in the late 1940s to the 1960s.   *$19.95 paperback. ISBN 1-894898-25-7*

Canmore and Kananaskis Country
by Gillean Daffern

The best hiking guide for anyone, regardless of skill level, who is interested in experiencing the vast and beautiful Kananaskis country.
$21.95 paperback. ISBN 1-894765-41-9

Ask for these great books at your local bookstore, or visit www.heritagehouse.ca